The Dream of Being

The Dream of Being

How an Ordinary Person Found Enlightenment

LOIS GIANCOLA

Copyright © by Lois Giancola

Published and distributed in the United States by Lois Giancola

This book was co-authored and edited by Bobi Conn.

All rights reserved. No part of this book may be reproduced by any mechanical, photographic, or electronic process, or in the form of a phonographic recording; nor may it be stored in a retrieval system, transmitted, or otherwise be copied for public or private use—other than for "fair use" as brief quotations embodied in articles and reviews—without prior written permission of the publisher.

The authors of this book do not dispense medical advice or prescribe the use of any technique as a form of treatment for physical, emotional, or medical problems without the advice of a physician, either directly or indirectly. The information in this book is intended to encourage and support individuals in their quests for spiritual meaning and purpose-driven lives. Your decision to utilize any of the modalities or practices described in this book is your choice, and the authors assume no responsibility for any consequences that may arise from said choices. The purpose of this book is to spread a message of hope and love, and we hope it succeeds in doing that.

Giancola, Lois.
The dream of being: how an ordinary person found enlightenment / Lois Giancola.
ISBN 1452892822
1. Body, Mind & Spirit. 2. Inspiration & Personal Growth.

ISBN: 1452892822
EAN-13: 9781452892825

1st edition, June 2010
Printed in the United States of America

*This book is dedicated to Larry Giancola—
husband, friend, and partner
on our journey!*

*"True love begins when nothing is looked for
in return." ~ Antoine de Saint-Exupery*

I Know Something Good About You

Wouldn't this old world be better,
If the folks we meet would say,
'I know something good about you',
And then treat us just that way.

Wouldn't it be fine and dandy,
If each handclasp warm and true,
Carried with it this assurance,
'I know something good about you'.

Wouldn't things here be more pleasant,
If the good that's in all,
Were the only things about us,
That folks bothered to recall.

Wouldn't life be lots more happy,
If we'd praise the good we see,
For there's such a lot of goodness,
In the worst of you and me.

Wouldn't it be nice to practice,
This fine way of thinking too--
'You know something good about me,
I know something good about you!'

~Author unknown~

Contents

Foreword xi

Chapter 1 1

Chapter 2 11

Chapter 3 19

Chapter 4 27

Chapter 5 33

Chapter 6 39

Chapter 7 59

Chapter 8 67

Chapter 9 83

Chapter 10 103

Chapter 11 113

Chapter 12 121

Chapter 13 147

Chapter 14 153

Spreading the Light 159

About the Author 193

"This place is a dream. Only a sleeper considers it real. Then death comes like dawn, and you wake up laughing at what you thought was your grief." ~Rumi

* Foreword *

Saturday, January 26, 2008: I just received a phone call from a co-worker; she confirmed that the information I gave her earlier this week turned out to be accurate. What really surprised her is that the information came to me from the voice of her deceased father, and this was not the first time I have heard messages from the other side.

What can a person do with this ability? I have been asking myself this question for years now. My knowingness tells me to write this book and then, I will *know*. Here I am, pecking away at my keyboard, listening to the guidance that comes to me, to the words that are spoken to me.

The Dream of Being

Several years ago, I was a different person—an angry person. I was filled with self-hatred and I lashed out both aloud and silently toward everyone around me. I couldn't control the criticism, disgust and judgment that seemed to determine my thoughts, my body language, and even the eye contact I made with people. I felt terrible about my constant negativity, but didn't know how to stop myself. How could such a thing happen? How could I be so controlled by a pattern, despise that pattern and not know I had the power to change it?

The answer is that I was acting from the programming I was taught by the most influential people in my life—my parents. *Mind programming*—was I a mere reflection of the programming I had learned as a child, through lessons that were sometimes obvious, but often subtle?

Of course I was. I was taught on a daily basis to distrust myself and others, to hate the world around me because it held nothing but danger and deceit. I gave up on the world just as I gave up on myself. I despised us all equally… I was programmed that way.

You may be asking yourself if this happened to you. The answer is yes—it happened to all of us.

Foreword

And despite the pain and the fear I felt, I found my way out and continue to this day to fight my robotic programming. It hasn't always been easy, but it is the most gratifying undertaking, the most fulfilling work I've experienced in this lifetime. Once I began to find my way and create my new, free self, I have discovered how to connect to the one true source of all wisdom—the energy of the universe around and throughout all of us, which some call God. I now rely on that wisdom with the knowingness of complete trust.

As I struggled out of my living nightmare, I looked around me and saw that all of my relationships had been based on a sense of self that I disliked. My children, my husband, co-workers, friends—at some point, I had viewed all of these people through my criticizing and fearful perception of the world. As that perception slowly gave way to something more beautiful, something peaceful and fulfilling, I saw everyone around me differently. My relationships changed as I changed; some grew stronger, but the ones that did not serve my growth fell away. Where everyone around me had reflected my inner hell before, they began to reflect my new sense of compassion.

The Dream of Being

I had always projected my inner self outwardly, but now I saw them as the spiritual beings that we all are.

I began my transformation in a moment of despair. As Neale Donald Walsch says, "All challenges are a sign of spiritual strength, and of the readiness of the Soul to move on; to evolve even further."

As you read this book, I pray you find your way out of any prison your mind has created, and free yourself from any limiting programming, as we are all put here to do.

Chapter 1

The Robotic Years

My previous life, from the age of eight to forty-two, was my own personal hellhole. I had very little self-esteem and thought that no matter what I did, I did the wrong thing. No matter what kind of effort I made, it was never good enough. Even if I somehow thought I was right about something, I needed to have that confirmed by others because I was programmed not to trust my own decisions or choices. As a child, I was unable to speak and share my feelings; as a result, I was called "backwards" and shy.

The Dream of Being

When I was twelve years old, I visited a friend's home with my parents. There were other children playing in the back yard and my parents encouraged me to play with them. I watched the kids enjoying themselves, seeming carefree and having fun. They looked nice, dressed in the latest styles. At that time, I didn't have stylish clothes or an abundance of any clothing, so I wore whatever was clean of my few outfits. However, I was not as alienated by the other kids' clothes as I was by their sense of freedom. They were perfectly comfortable with themselves and accepting of each other. Those concepts were foreign to me and I only grew more uncomfortable as I stood there watching them.

Instead of feeling free to do what felt right to me, I had been programmed to try to determine if everyone around me would approve of what I did—and I especially needed to be sure my parents would approve. I was constantly dancing an intricate emotional and psychological dance, but even if I had an extra set of legs, I never could have done it well enough to please my parents or myself.

Chapter 1

The adults urged me to go play, and the other parents watched me with questioning eyes, as if they knew that something was wrong inside me, but they didn't know how to help. My parents, on the other hand, became more and more angry with me as I stood there, frozen. As the adults tried to convince me to go play, I felt increasingly paralyzed, as if their attention was too much to bear. My self-consciousness kept me from responding at all, and I could only visualize myself somehow failing if I tried to be a child like the other children—I would fall down, I would drop a slice of cake, I would spill the lemonade. Everyone would see my inadequacies and mock me.

Another parent had the children come ask me to play, as if mere shyness was the problem. When I remained frozen, my Father grabbed my arm and jerked me from where I stood, saying, "What in the hell is wrong with you?" When I heard his disdain and annoyance, the tears began streaming down my face. At this point, I felt that everyone was staring, and whether they did or not, I assumed they were laughing at me, too.

The more I cried, the more I wondered what was wrong with me. Was I mentally disturbed? Why was I the only kid acting this way? I felt powerless and overwhelmed—the defining qualities of my childhood.

At the age of forty-nine, I finally understand why I felt so powerless that day and why I could not interact in the ways society expected me to. My power was taken from me at the age of eight, when I was sexually molested.

On a dreary Sunday afternoon, someone I loved and trusted took my innocence from me and betrayed my trust. The light was dim but the scene remains vivid in my mind. Clothes lay on the tile floor and clutter sat on the bedroom furniture. I was assured that there was nothing wrong while my clothes were removed and my hands were guided to places and body parts I never knew existed. Lies were told to gain access to my most private places, and threats issued to ensure that I would never tell anyone what happened, afraid of the punishment I would receive.

When I left the room, sickness washed over me and my mind went into shock. I felt the dirtiness like an open wound that wept profusely. My vow of secrecy and knowing that what had happened was wrong unleashed my mental hell. Do I tell my Mother? Will she protect me and rescue me from the anguish? Or will she punish me, full of wrath that I allowed this to happen?

Ultimately, I did not feel safe enough to tell my Mother, and I chose to endure the anguish of my private hell rather than risk her fury. I tolerated my own relentless judgments and did not risk her damnation.

The events of that Sunday afternoon and the others that followed impacted every day of my life as I found myself living a nightmare in the hell of my mind that I never could have imagined.

To this point, home was a place where I felt safe, and I always looked forward to returning there. I especially enjoyed going home after being at school all day because I could see the person who meant the most to me in life—my Mother. Seeing her reassured me that everything was safe and secure. For a short time during my young life, she worked and wasn't home when I arrived from school, which was unsettling and odd. We weren't allowed to leave the house until she arrived, and life only seemed safe when she was there.

I was accustomed to coming home, changing into play clothes, and going back outside to roam my neighborhood.

The Dream of Being

On a particularly sunny afternoon, I stepped into the house and saw a look on my Mother's face that I had never seen before. Her eyes were wild and flashed with anger. Jaws clenched, she grabbed my arm and dragged me through the house to her bedroom, my books falling to the floor. She pulled me into her bedroom, slammed the door behind us, and unleashed her fury on me with the leather belt she had grabbed. The pain of the first blows quickly sank in and I leapt onto the bed on all fours, desperately trying to get out of her reach.

The rage on her face erupted through her voice as she began screaming at me, demanding to know how I could have done such a thing. Her eyes were cold and piercing, as if she wanted me dead at that moment. With tears of anger streaming down her face, she thundered that I was going straight to **hell**. I was to go to Confession as soon as possible and tell the priest about what I had done, how I had sinned, but neither I nor my siblings could leave the yard to play.

I never made a sound, and she did not offer any explanation or ask for mine. I was shaking and my tears were ready to spill over. My judge and jury, she watched me slink along the edges of the room, my back to the walls, so I could leave through her bedroom door and run to my bedroom on the second floor of our Cape Cod home.

On that day, the world as I had known it changed forever. Convinced that I was going to hell, I trembled inside, knowing that I was doomed to suffer for an eternity. I began enacting my own demise. Believing that I was lower than the lowliest garbage on earth, I expected to be treated as such from then on.

I lay in bed awake for several nights, wondering what to say to the priest. My parents presented themselves as the most righteous parents who walked the earth, and they thought themselves to be so. What would the priest think if he recognized me? My parents constantly pointed out the faults of others in comparison to their own piety. According to my Mother, I had committed a mortal sin, and there was no hope for me.

She hounded me every day, wanting to know if I had gone to Confession. The priests weren't always available, and at the age of eight it was difficult for me to figure out when I should go. I realized, though, that life at my house was going to be unbearable until I did, so I went as soon as

I could. I remember that event as vividly as if it happened yesterday. I kneeled in the confessional, waiting apprehensively for the priest to arrive. I was filled with turmoil, wondering what to say when he slid open the small window between us to hear what I had to say. Should I tell him exactly what happened, or should I make it seem less than it was so he wouldn't think badly of my family? In the end, I spoke softly and gave a vague account of what happened, as my concern for my family's honor was so stringently ingrained in me. I felt relieved that I could tell my Mother I had gone to Confession, but I felt no better about myself. I fully believed that I deserved to be condemned, that I was worthless as a human being, since I had been a part of something so disgusting.

No one ever asked me what happened, spoke with me about it, or tried to see how I was feeling inside. My Mother had already exploded; my Dad just looked at me with disgust. One evening soon after her full and unwavering rejection, I tried to climb onto my Father's lap. After I raised one leg up, he pushed me away and said, "Don't touch me after what you did."

Chapter 1

I turned away and my head hung down, tears filling my eyes. I ran up the stairs to my bedroom and threw myself on my bed. I lay there sobbing alone, feeling as if I had just been pushed off of a tightrope and was falling through space with no one to protect me—not even the two people I was supposed to trust the most in my life, whom I was taught to trust *with* my life. I had unconsciously believed they would love me always and unconditionally—now I was abandoned.

Chapter 2

After that day in my Mother's bedroom, I began to lose my sense of self. The strength of my spirit slipped away and I felt no reason for staying alive on this earth. My confidence was shattered and my grades at school suffered. I hung my head everywhere I went, full of shame and self-loathing. Thankfully, I did have three friends who supported me during that time. Without them, I do not believe that I would be alive today. I thank them for being the angels they were to me. None of them ever knew what had happened or any part of my drama, as my Mother had mandated complete silence. After witnessing and feeling the sting of her wrath the first time, I would never cross that line.

I began to withdraw from my siblings, since I was emotionally estranged from my parents. I was the youngest of six children, with two eldest sisters and three brothers in the middle. Looking back, I can see that they all had their individual dramas they were trying to process. They were all just trying to survive the programming our parents drilled into us, and our parents were products of their time. They were doing exactly what had been passed down to them by their own German parents.

I also spent every moment I could away from my home. It became the last place where I wanted to be, so I escaped to my friends' homes to play Daniel Boone or to play with dolls—anything to temporarily leave the hellhole of my mind. At that time, kids would just yell outside a friend's house, "Suzy, can you come out to play?" If she could, the adults would send her outside to play. If not, someone would come and say the kid wasn't home. I would start at the top of my list with my favorite friends, and work my way down to the least-likable kid in the neighborhood—even they were suitable playmates in a pinch. I befriended some of the elderly people in our neighborhood and would visit with them sometimes. I felt safe in everyone's home except my own.

After what my Mother had done, I felt as if I could do nothing right. Even if I had been the perfect child, I was always convinced that I was fully wrong in every way. At the age of nine or ten, we had a graduation party at our house and all of our relatives sat in a circle in our front yard, sharing in conversation. I walked past them to go to the back yard and play as a caterer began delivering food for the party. One of my uncles said, "Lois, go carry that tray for that man," so I rushed to the older gentleman and said, "Let me carry that for you." He looked at me and said, "Honey, you can't carry this. It is too heavy." My uncle burst out laughing at this exchange, and I turned a bright red and ran to the back yard. I could hear him saying "I embarrassed her" with delight.

Every day of my life felt like that event. I tried my best to do as I was told or to do what I thought was best and always, someone would pull the rug out from under me.

The Dream of Being

    My trust in people, and especially in my Mother, was shattered even further again when I was eight. One evening after supper, I went to play at a business construction site behind a neighbor's house. All of my friends went there to watch the work and play, as it was a new development in the neighborhood. I climbed the neighbor's fence and saw my two friends. I went to them, happy to find someone I knew, and asked them to play in the dirt with me. They said they had to go home to eat dinner and left with their older brother. I played in the dirt by myself for a short time and when I turned around, I saw a man looking at me. He motioned for me to come to him but since I had never seen him before, I continued to play in the dirt. I began feeling uneasy and looked up again; he motioned for me to come to him again, then began walking toward me.

    Something inside me told me to run, so I jumped up from my crouching position and ran toward my neighbor's fence. I cleared it in one leap and ran all the way home, not knowing if he followed me or not because I never turned to look. My Mother was reading the newspaper in the living room. When I told her what happened, she told me not to leave the house for the rest of the evening.

Sometime between 8:00 and 9:00 that evening, our doorbell rang—it was one of our neighbors looking for their sister. I went outside with my family to help look for her and shortly after returning home, I saw her run down the hill and through her front door. I ran to her house up the street from mine and through her open door, saw her in her mother's arms. She had been raped by a man that she met at the construction site; he was a patron at the old establishment that they were replacing.

Later in the week, at supper time, the Chief of Police came to our front door and spoke with my parents. My Father was the mayor of our small town at this time, so he had passed along the story I had told my Mother about the man I saw. My Mother called me away from the meal, took me into the family bathroom, and closed the door. She showed me a picture of a man and asked me if he was the man who had chased me. The man in the picture had medium-length, sandy blonde hair, unlike the man I had seen. I told her that it was not him, that the man I saw had dark, short hair and was not as handsome as the one in the picture.

She opened the bathroom door and went back to our front door, where she told the Chief of Police *yes, it was the same man.* Dumbfounded, I returned to my seat at the table and never again spoke about this incident with my Mother. During the trial, the sandy-haired man was killed in an automobile accident. This man whom my Mother accused had actually raped my friend, but I did not understand at the time how she could lie about my experience to ensure he was caught. I learned again that I could not trust anyone in this world.

I was taught that the world is an unsafe place once again when I was eight. In his position as the mayor of our town, my Father did something that somehow upset a motorcycle gang in the area. He was told that they were going to come to our house and burn it down on a night when our Mother happened to be having surgery. Our Father told us we could play in the back yard but not to leave it, and not to turn any lights on inside the house. He walked around with a handgun at his side, which I had never seen him do before.

Chapter 2

He had explained the situation to the two eldest sisters but told them not to tell us younger kids. Of course we could tell that something strange was going on, so we asked persistent questions until someone finally told us. The motorcycle gang never showed up, but I never again felt safe to sleep in my home.

* Chapter 3 *

There is a saying that time heals all wounds. I don't believe this is an accurate understanding of pain. What happens instead is that over time, one develops survival techniques to mask and protect what is unhealed. As more time elapsed after the most traumatic events of my childhood, I would do anything to avoid thinking about what had happened. I had so much self-doubt that I became a puppet, acting in accordance with other people's expectations, rather than making any decisions of my own and taking the risk of being wrong.

I knew that life was safer that way, without ever again feeling the kind of rage my Mother directed toward me for being "wrong." If I pleased everyone, I wouldn't feel my Father's disappointment again. If someone belittled me or triggered my feelings of inferiority, I would simply run from the situation.

I had so much damnation and doom lurking within my subconscious mind that I could not have looked at myself and my pain directly at that time—my mind could not handle it. Instead, I kept my own awareness of my pain on the periphery; as long as I didn't acknowledge it directly, I could survive.

But while the conscious mind can be fooled, the subconscious mind cannot. Though I fought against the truth of what had happened and I resisted thinking about it, my subconscious mind would not let it go completely ignored.

As a teenager, I began to sleepwalk. As soon as I would close my eyes and fall asleep, I would see my house burning around me. That image was so clear that I can still see it now, some forty years later. Each time I "saw" the house in flames, I would get out of bed and rush out of my bedroom, telling everyone I found that the house was burning. At first, whoever was in the house would tell me that everything was okay, that the house was not on fire. The more I did it, the more amusing everyone found it. I am sure I would have found it funny if one of my siblings had been doing it instead of me.

But today, I realize that my mind was living in the hell and damnation that my Mother had sent me to with her words. I believed that I was not worthy of her love, my Father's love, or the love and forgiveness of God. I could find no peace in my mind and spent my school years feeling fragile. The friendliness I felt as a child faded away and was replaced by my doubt and loathing.

The one thing that I did continue to succeed in was athletics. As far back as I can remember, I could compete with males and females alike and either win or come close to it. This way of achieving allowed me to subconsciously hold onto something positive about myself, a little shred of evidence that I was still worthwhile. I would win races at picnics, and play softball, dodgeball, football—any game with the neighborhood kids. It seemed that I could achieve anything I wanted physically, but nothing mentally.

I played volleyball at school in the eighth grade and was pretty good at it. When I became a freshman in high school, I decided to join the team. I went to the gym for tryouts on the day one of my classmates told me they were being held, but nobody was there. Immediately, I berated myself for being wrong again. I assumed that my classmate had lied to me so I wouldn't make the team, since I would have succeeded if I just had the chance. She was one of the school's top female athletes, and I let my anger toward her and my humiliation keep me from pursuing a place on the team. Since I never discussed any of my interests or desires with my parents, there was no one to encourage me to keep trying.

High school as a whole was an unsettling time for me. I had a handful of friends, each planning their future direction in life, and as the years progressed, I became more self-critical and more judgmental. I didn't really trust anyone. I did have one "best friend" at this time and a few other friends, but no longer were my peers accepting and flexible like we were as children. As teenagers, it seemed that everyone besides me was sure of what they wanted and who they were. If someone didn't fit into a particular group and have well-defined common interests, there was no room for that person to join in. No longer could we all play make-believe together, regardless of our differences. If someone stood out as being different, they were generally treated with indifference.

If my best friend was sick at home or on a field trip, I went through the entire day without any social contact. I would stand alone during our breaks, wander around by myself, and eventually find myself standing in a corner of the building, asking myself, "Why am I not good enough to have anyone else in my life?" I never tried to make new friends because any time I thought of it, my conscious mind quickly shut me down with a disdainful, "Who would want you?" My own mind kept me from reaching for anything I ever wanted, though I wouldn't see that until much later in life. Though I felt weak, my mind was incredibly powerful—it controlled me in every situation, paralyzing me and rendering me helpless.

Dealing with the opposite sex was even more difficult than trying to have friendships. I could hardly even look at boys or men. Each time I would walk into a convenience store, if I saw that the clerk was male, I would hold my head down, staring at the floor so that I couldn't see the disgust I knew was in his eyes. Even if he didn't notice me or was trying to be kind, I wouldn't have noticed, so overwhelmed with guilt and self-hatred I was. It was as if there was a news ticker from the television playing through my mind with a constant feed: *You are going to Hell. You are a piece of shit. You are disgusting. How dare you do something so horrible? Nobody will ever want you!*

If, for some reason, I did end up talking to a man or a boy, my face immediately turned beet red. That was my scarlet letter, which I wore on my face for the world to see; it was a neon sign flashing my shame to the world. Every time, I subconsciously told every male I spoke to, "I did something bad and should be punished, so I am not worthy of your attention!" All of those conversations ended quickly, with me rushing out the door. If any of my friends witnessed it, they would tell me that I was a snob and that I must have thought I was better than everyone else. It was the farthest thing from the truth. I understand why they thought so, but my shutting people out had everything to do with how I felt about myself and nothing to do with how I felt about them.

When my senior year of high school came, I decided that I wanted to attend the prom so I could feel normal and be a part of something my classmates were doing. I asked my Mom and she said that I could go only if I went with my friend's brother. I felt incredible! I was so excited to be doing something that would make me feel like everyone else. My friend and I decided to ask our brothers to go with one another, and they both agreed to. I was so excited the night of the prom—I thought that it would be the highlight of my life.

Both of us couples went to the prom together. When we arrived at the school gym, we found seats and proceeded to spend almost the entire night sitting. It was terribly awkward for us to be in that situation together, everyone knowing each other but us friends being with each other's brother. Lines were drawn and walls went up; nobody felt comfortable. Worse yet, our dates did not want to dance because they lacked both the knowledge and the confidence in that setting. The day after the prom, we all attended a school function at a local park. Somehow, it was worse than the prom itself. We were all glad when that weekend was over—what I had thought would be the best time of my life.

* Chapter 4 *

When I graduated from high school, I landed a temporary job through a hiring agency at an insurance company. There I would receive a social education outside of the Catholic schools I had attended, away from the watchful monitoring of my parents. I was one of four office staff in a company with about twenty-five insurance agents. We were of all ages, and most of my co-workers were men. I still remember my first day there.

Each reporting morning, the agents would turn in their paperwork and the money they had collected from customers. I sat at a collection window and was introduced

The Dream of Being

to each agent who stepped up to process their paperwork. I could feel my face flashing red with each introduction, and I knew that they could tell I was embarrassed when they politely smiled or nodded at me.

After working with the company for a few months, I grew more comfortable and began to find my voice. This, of course, was a new development for me and I was excited to be able to express myself openly. I can look back and see that I was being sarcastic and degrading to others at times, but during that time in my life, I was focused only on how free I felt, not having someone to constantly hush me or tell me I should have spoken differently. Though I was obnoxious at times, I was blissfully ignorant, reveling in my newfound freedom.

The insurance company soon hired me as their full-time employee, and I stayed there for the next nine years. The strict regime and mind control of my home and school life slowly loosened their grip. Just being in a different environment allowed me to feel much more free, despite the fact that my Mother still tried to control me when I was home. My Mother took my first eight paychecks and beginning with the ninth paycheck, I was to purchase a cheap car to get back and forth to work. I decided to hide everything from her regarding my work life and co-workers, fearing she would somehow take this taste of freedom away from me. She was constantly interrogating me and could punish me with guilt at any time. She kept her vice-like grip on me with a barrage of mind control tactics whenever I was in her presence.

Away from her, though, I was surrounded by people who didn't at all share her strict ideas and judgments of others. I began to observe these individuals whose lives were so different from my own—some of them were religious, but some of them didn't go to church. Some of them used others to get what they wanted, but there were also some who cared about me, even after they got to know me. I realized that I had qualities people liked and didn't like. It was all very different from what I had experienced for the first eighteen years of my life.

This environment allowed me to try on different personas and explore who I really wanted to be. I had never considered my own desires about who I wanted to be in the past; I always had someone to tell me what I should and shouldn't be, and if I went against that, they had convinced me that there was something wrong with me. The first issue that always came to my mind in making decisions was the fear of going to hell. I began observing others carefully to see how they handled various situations. If their words or actions seemed right to me, I imitated them in my own life. When I saw a person make someone else feel good, I adopted their personality trait that was attractive to others.

As I did this, I began to make and keep new friends. It was an incredible, simple process that allowed me to finally see that others could appreciate and enjoy *me*. It felt so wonderful to be accepted, wanted, and loved by others that I observed just about everyone, using my adoption techniques to form a better and better self. In this new game that I was playing, if I ran into someone who didn't like me or who wasn't receptive to me, I didn't waste my time with them. I was either mean or dismissive to the people who didn't give me the attention I craved and constantly sought. Looking back, I realize that I just could not handle any more rejection or criticism in my life, and I didn't want to take any chances with people who might find something to dislike about me. What I was experiencing was like having candy for the first time in my life—it tasted so good, and I never again wanted to live without it.

Chapter 5

When I was eighteen, I had my first experience ever with dating. My best friend JoAnn and I had been going to a dance club called Guys 'N Dolls regularly. My sisters, who were eight and nine years older than me, had told me about the place. It had a minimum age requirement of twenty-one, but JoAnn's cousins told us that the people at the door didn't check I.D.s, so we gave it a shot and became regulars. I had never done something that my Mom wouldn't approve of, but this definitely would have fallen into that category. I felt daring, though, and the more I went, the easier it became, and my guilt faded.

The Dream of Being

JoAnn was the all-American girl—blue eyes and naturally blonde hair. Her hair wasn't just a little blonde, but so light that it almost looked white when it was bleached out by the summer sun. She had a perfect figure that any red-blooded American boy would have found attractive. I had reddish-brown hair, hazel eyes, and was built like a stick. I was 5'10" with no curves and not the standard of beauty.

One Friday night, two boys strutted to the booth we occupied. They had a spring in their steps and a deliberate cocky air to them. They asked if they could join us and plopped right down. They were obviously confident and used to meeting girls. I had never been in a situation like this before, and we all sat around talking, enjoying ourselves. After a few minutes, it was clear that the boy next to JoAnn had been the one wanting to come to our table to meet her. I still couldn't keep my eyes off of him. By the end of the conversation, JoAnn and Larry had made a date for the next night. Larry looked at Don sitting next to me and asked him, "Why don't you two meet us at Pic's tomorrow night?" Don, in turn, asked me if I wanted to go out the next night. Even though he was obviously

Chapter 5

reluctant, I was thrilled at this prospect of a new adventure and jumped at the chance. Trying to conceal my excitement, I casually said, "Sure. What time?"

And I was ecstatic. My first real date was now planned, and my head was spinning at the idea that someone was willing to go on a date with *me*! I was actually good enough for someone to willingly go on a date with me—someone accepted me and was willing to let the world see it. I couldn't sleep that night and could hardly wait for him to pick me up the next evening. He was going to pick me up, and then he was going to take me somewhere in *public*. In the back of my mind, though, I knew that I didn't deserve this kindness—I was a disgusting person who was going to hell. Who was I to think I could be around other people, especially those who were obviously so much better than me?

Don picked me up around 7:00 on Saturday night, and we met Larry and JoAnn at Pic's Café, where we played pool and had a few drinks. I didn't know how to handle situations like these, so I was quiet and observed everyone else. After about an hour and a half, JoAnn wanted to go home, but I didn't know why at the time. The next day, she said that she didn't like the way Larry talked to her and the kind of language he used, so she wanted nothing to do with him. My date continued calling me after that night and we dated for the next several months.

Dating Don was a whirlwind of internal battles for me. I had learned that anything that felt good was wrong, so I was always arguing with my own mind about what to do, what not to do. I had never kissed anyone before him, so that turned into quite the fiasco. At the age of eighteen, I would overhear talk about other people—this one was a good kisser, that one was a bad kisser, and so on. I wasn't sure what it took to be a good kisser, so I did my best but later heard that I always bit his lip. I never knew that I was doing it, but managed to somehow.

Every time we were alone, Don wanted to make out with me. All that making out sparked sensations in my body that I had never felt before. It felt wonderful, but I constantly told myself that if I did anything other than kiss him, I would have no chance of getting out of hell. By this time, I had convinced myself that if I prayed hard enough, I might be able to convince God to let me go, to forgive me. That was the flicker of hope I held onto and which every person needs in this world to maintain some degree of mental stability.

I'm sure that Don was often frustrated, considering my perception of myself and our relationship at the time. One Sunday, he invited me to an outing and told me that one of his old girlfriends would be there. I went, but I was so trapped in the hellhole of my mind that I hardly spoke a word. I was intimidated, but worse yet, I started telling myself that Don didn't want me anymore, that he wanted his old girlfriend back. I felt frozen, taking this event to be an affirmation of my worst fears—that I wasn't and would never be good enough for anyone.

Another evening, I was dressed for a graduation party at Don's house and was waiting for him to pick me up. I came out of my bedroom and into the living room, where my Mother was reading the newspaper. She looked at me around the newspaper and told me, "You aren't leaving the house with that on." A wave of shame washed over me immediately, as I automatically assumed that I had chosen the wrong clothes to wear because deep inside, I was nothing but a tramp. The offensive item was clearly my tank top, which I wore with jeans. I went into my room and put a white blouse over it. "Now you're talking," she said, looking over the paper.

I knew that what I was wearing, then and in general, was conservative compared to what most eighteen year-olds were wearing, but it seemed that I could do no right in my Mother's eyes. Her constant criticism fed the turmoil inside me, as I became more and more frustrated at always being wrong. By the time Don picked me up, I was once again so caught up in my mental hell that I couldn't enjoy the party. People talked to me and were trying to be nice, but I was so self-conscious that I didn't notice their efforts. I thought that everyone must have noticed my tank top and knew that once again, I made a horrible choice in life that revealed me for the piece of shit I was.

Chapter 6

After that summer, Don moved away to go to college and my life moved in another direction. Though I'm sure that he thought I acted strangely at times, Don and I never argued or had disagreements. He called me occasionally from college and I would see him when he visited home. JoAnn and I kept going to Guys 'N Dolls, and I saw Larry there almost every time. JoAnn didn't speak to him much after their hour-and-a-half date, but that never stopped him from sitting down at our table and talking to us, and particularly to me.

Eventually, JoAnn began dating another Don—Don S.—who was friends with Larry and the first Don. Larry would sit with me and we would talk for most of the night while JoAnn and Don S. danced or went outside to be alone. Getting to know Larry opened up a whole new world for me. Larry would pick out a girl, then bet me that she would dance with him and let him kiss her. I always lost because I never saw a girl turn him down or get upset about him making his move.

As time went on, Larry started talking to me about his family and how he felt about things in his life, especially his father's wrath. Larry and I slowly and very comfortably became friends. During this time, he dated other girls and at times didn't spend as much time talking with me. I could feel a connection between us, though. The first night I met him, I wished he had asked me to dance when he asked JoAnn. I never thought I was good enough for a man as charming as Larry, and I was awed by his confidence and cockiness—he would do and try anything for the sake of enjoying himself, and everyone around him could tell that he knew how to live life. He could steer any situation into a negative or positive direction, depending on his mood, and Larry was almost always brewing some excitement somewhere.

Chapter 6

Months went by with me seeing Don off and on, all while watching Larry and his off-and-on dates. One Friday afternoon, Don called me to tell me that he didn't want to date me anymore. I called JoAnn to tell her, and she said that her boyfriend had already told her about Don's plan to end our relationship. He also told her that Don had been coming back on the weekends and was dating someone else. And finally, she knew that Don was going to be at our hangout that night with his new girlfriend. My heart sank. My mind began its usual attack on me: I didn't deserve him, I never had deserved him. I wasn't good enough for him or anyone else, and I might as well get used to being alone.

Looking back, I always knew that my relationship with Don wasn't going anywhere; I dated him because nobody else wanted me. I never entertained thoughts about what I wanted or what was good for me—that was never part of my programming. I only allowed others to manipulate and control me because I didn't realize that I had any power—not even power over my own thoughts. Most importantly, I didn't know that I was *allowed* to have that power. It had never occurred to me that I owned any part of myself and had the right to enjoy it and use it for my own happiness.

JoAnn and I had already made plans to go to Guys 'N Dolls on this particular Saturday, and backing out was not an option. We arrived before any of the guys, and I knew that they were there when Don S. came up to JoAnn and asked her to dance. I sat in a booth and as they danced, I glanced to the right of them and saw Don with his new girlfriend, slow-dancing and in the middle of an unrestrained French kiss. I was both disgusted and uncomfortable, so I stood up to go to the bathroom.

As I turned away from that scene, I saw Larry strolling straight toward me, wearing his characteristic cocky smirk. Without saying a word, he held his hand out toward me and took hold of mine. He led me to the dance floor and for the first time since I was eight years old, I felt safe again. I didn't notice anything else for the rest of the night—Larry and I danced and it was as if the rest of the club had disappeared into a fog. From that night forward, Larry and I were dating. I found out later that Don had asked Larry to keep an eye on me while he was at school.

Chapter 6

That request of his was the best gift I have ever received from any person—Larry did an excellent job!

My life completely changed after that night. Being with Larry showed me a completely different perspective on life. His home life was pretty much the complete opposite of mine. There was nothing that went unsaid in Larry's house; nothing was taboo or inappropriate. I was used to not talking about a number of things and topics that I implicitly knew were never to be spoken. Larry did all the things that I had been told not to do—drinking, smoking pot, speeding, fighting, cussing, going to strip clubs—living life on the edge. He never hesitated to say exactly what was on his mind. But as I had gotten to know Larry at Guys 'N Dolls, I also saw a gentle, caring, loving, and troubled young man. A lot of people dismissed him for his arrogant and brazen personality, but I had seen something else that resided deep inside him.

Before long, I began to experience the roller coaster inside Larry. Several months after we began dating, I went on a summer vacation with a girlfriend. When I returned, Larry came to my house and told me that he had dated a co-worker while I was in Florida and he wanted to break up with me. His reasoning, he said, was that I had probably met and hung out with other guys while I was on vacation, but I hadn't—in fact, I had refused to spend time with other guys.

Once again, I felt like I was free-falling. I had lost the only safe person in my world, and I no longer had anyone I could trust. I didn't say anything to him as he dumped the news on me. After he left, I fell back into my old self-disgust: Nobody would ever want me. The feelings I had felt were too good for me. How dare I think I could finally feel good about myself?

I didn't see Larry very much after we broke up. Months passed by and JoAnn continued to date Don S. We would frequent different dance clubs and one weekday night, JoAnn picked me up and told me she wanted to see if Don was at Pic's Café. We drove the 25 minutes from Erlanger to Newport, Kentucky, and recognized a car outside the café. JoAnn went inside to find Don and came back out with him. She asked me to go inside the café and hang out with Larry while she and Don went somewhere alone. I never expressed how I felt to anyone—I just did what was asked of me because I was afraid of upsetting

Chapter 6

people and losing them as friends. I was scared to death to walk through the doors of this bar and to see Larry once again. I knew that I was still crazy about him, but I was afraid of seeing a look of disgust on his face for intruding on his home away from home. That's what Pic's Café meant to him.

When I stepped into the café, I saw Larry's sparkling dark eyes and his charming smile. He started talking to me and almost immediately, was begging me to go back out with him. I couldn't reply—I was in complete shock. I couldn't believe that someone who had known me actually wanted me back in his life! My programming was telling me to act indignant as a way to punish him for hurting me before. My heart, though, told me to grab him and tell him how much I had missed him. I said nothing; I just listened.

He told me how much he missed me and that he had realized he loved me. An older gentleman at the bar joined in our conversation and told me that Larry loved and missed me—he had spoken of me often to this man. I was overwhelmed with emotion and about to burst with excitement, having *two* people trying to convince me to take Larry back. I felt so lucky, since I knew I couldn't possibly be worthy of so much attention. After a while, I told Larry I would give him one more chance. When I laid my head on my pillow that night, I knew that sleep would never come—I relived that scene from the bar over and over.

Larry and I continued to date, and the more time I spent with him, the more I understood what a free spirit he was. I also began to see how self-absorbed I was, wracked with guilt and a constant stream of self-criticism. We attended an annual dance in January with Larry's family and friends. My Mother had given me permission to spend the night at his married sister's house afterwards. She agreed because she understood that Larry would not be spending the night there, but he did. While kissing me in front of the television, Larry asked me to marry him and I said YES!

After we became engaged, Larry and I had many conversations in which I lined out all of my demands in order to marry him. He would have to go to church with me every Sunday; we wouldn't have sex until we were married; we'd use natural methods for childbearing; he wouldn't go out drinking in bars; he wouldn't do this, he wouldn't do that. Larry agreed to everything I shoved down his throat, and told me everything I wanted to hear. I knew, though, that he didn't agree with any of it, and he never required anything of me. He had anger inside him, though, that made him very gruff sometimes. He would sometimes respond in ways that seemed to suck the energy right out of me.

Visiting his family's home gave me a lot of insight into Larry's world. He was constantly met with doubt, disappointment, distrust and negative comments. His dad always sounded disgusted with Larry and spoke aggressively toward him, ending every conversation with a discouraging comment. His mother doubted everything he said, and his siblings were critical of Larry.

I didn't realize it at the time, but Larry drew all of this negative behavior to himself. He desperately wanted his father's attention, and he had become the child who acts out to get negative attention. After all, if there is no positive attention to be had, a child will seek negative attention—the only option that is somehow better than no attention at all. Seeing Larry's pain made me feel my own pain more acutely, and I wanted to protect him. I thought that I had the right to protect him and that he deserved to be protected—things I never believed about myself. I lashed out at anyone who hurt him verbally as I would have liked to lash out at my own offenders. I could do for Larry what I couldn't do for myself, but at the time, using Larry as my crutch was the safest way for me to try out this new, important part of myself.

As our wedding date grew nearer, both of our families began expressing concerns about the marriage—they didn't think we should wed, and didn't think it would last. Larry's friends at Pic's Café placed bets on how long it would last—two years was the maximum. One Saturday evening, I visited Larry's mother while he was at a men-only function, and she asked me if I was sure that I wanted to marry him. She told me that he was "a handful," and not a truthful person. I looked straight at her and told her that I knew exactly who I was marrying.

On another evening, my oldest sister told me that I could do better than Larry and asked me to reconsider marrying him. My immediate reaction was to think that no one else would ever want me, so I wouldn't be able to "do better." No matter what anyone said, I was determined to marry the only person who I felt truly wanted me in his life.

The morning of the wedding, I went into the office to make sure that everything would run smoothly—by this time, I was the Office Manager at the insurance company. JoAnn went with me to Cincinnati, where it was located. We took I-75 back to Erlanger and as we drove down the exit ramp, a construction worker on the overpass dropped a board onto the ramp. JoAnn swerved her car and missed it, and we laughed about the close call on my wedding day.

She dropped me off at my house and we each went to the various appointments we had scheduled. I went to a hair salon and had my hair done. When the beautician finished, I looked in the mirror and felt a wave of disappointment. Somehow, I had thought that the person I saw in the mirror would be different that day—she wasn't. I saw myself and thought I was still looking at "yucky Lois." Before long, I began to cry. The hairdresser got upset that *I* was upset, but finally I accepted that she had done the best she could with what she had to work with. I would also be wearing a veil, so there was that to take into consideration.

The Dream of Being

    Back at my house, I began to prepare for the 7:00 p.m. wedding. Around 4:00, the photographer came and took pictures of me and my Mother in front of the living room windows. He had us looking into each other's eyes, which I found difficult to do. The anger inside of me seemed to well up as I looked straight at her, but I managed to keep it pushed down inside of me. The photographer also took pictures of me with my Father. The whole experience was very strange, interacting with my parents on such an intimate and personal level—it was terribly uncomfortable.

    As the youngest child in our family, I was now the only one left at home, so there wasn't a lot of hustle and bustle for my wedding. I rode with my parents to St. Henry's, our family church and where I had attended school for twelve years. I stayed in the back of the church until 7:00, waiting for the ceremony to begin.

    While I stood back there, and as I finally walked down the aisle to Larry, and even to the point where I said my vows, I asked myself if I really wanted to go through with it. I knew I was getting married for all the wrong reasons. I knew that I did not love Larry but cared for him more than anyone else in my life. I wanted to escape my home and be somewhere that felt safe. So I proceeded through the ceremony, knowing well that I was not strong enough to ever walk away.

When the ceremony ended, we went outside to have more pictures taken and then went to the church hall for the reception. There, a reception line formed and one by one, I greeted each of our guests. I felt distant as I thanked them, fully distracted by the uneasiness I had in social situations. I had never been taught any guidelines for socializing, and it wasn't something I had often done. After that, we went through the traditional wedding movements—cutting the cake, throwing the bouquet and garter, specified dances, and so on. That day and evening were unusually hot. It was May 11, and everyone had sweat pouring from them whether they were dancing or not. Larry's parents always did the jitterbug at every dance or party we attended, so it was fun to watch them do that at my own wedding.

When the evening ended, Larry and I went home to the mobile home we had purchased six months earlier. I was so scared—this would be the first sexual experience of my life since the molestation occurred. A host of emotions rose inside me, and I was glad when the night was over. The next morning, we drove to Gatlinburg, Tennessee to see the sites, the mountains, and, of course, all the shops. After several days, we returned home again.

At first, our honeymoon and new life felt forbidden and foreign to me. It seemed forbidden because it was the first time I ever lived with someone besides my parents, and the hierarchy of power that had kept me in my place was now gone. When the sense of freedom set in and I really understood there was no one to report to, I began taking on the role of my Mother. Looking back, I can see that while I hated the oppressive customs and expectations at my parents' house, that reality was all I knew, and I re-created it to give myself the sense of security the old regime had provided. All of their programming, orders, and rules were so embedded in me that it scared me not to have them in my life. I became the judge of my home, and made almost every decision about money, church, and our social environment. I suddenly felt superior to Larry and his habits—just like my Mother—and let that justify my need for control.

Chapter 6

Both before and after we were married, Larry's employment and dealings with money were an issue between us. Our arguments led to deceit, which in turn prompted my spiraling descent into once more believing that I had made the wrong choice in life by marrying Larry. It would take a long time for me to trust and to feel safe with him again. From what I had known and things that I heard, Larry had been employed as an orderly at a hospital and had also worked for a flooring business off and on before I knew him and while we dated. Prior to us getting married and on the day of our wedding, he was unemployed. I would leave for work every morning to my corporate position, leaving him sleeping in our bed. Whenever I confronted him about getting a job, he always had an excuse as to why he didn't have one and couldn't find one. When he did work, he changed jobs as if he were changing clothes.

This issue made me worry that it had been a mistake to marry him, so I did what my family had taught me to do when there was a potential problem: sweep it under the rug, and keep moving along. One Saturday morning, though, Larry's uncle called. He was a manager at a bank and asked about a loan in Larry's name that was in default. Earlier in the month, we had gotten a letter about that outstanding loan and Larry assured me it was his father's, since they shared the same name. I, in turn, told his uncle that it was his father's loan, not Larry's. His uncle had been the one to give Larry the loan, and told me that it was indeed my Larry, and not his father, who had taken out the loan and was in default.

I felt so betrayed once again by someone who was supposed to love me that I let the floodgates open and I let Larry's uncle hear my wrath. His uncle tried to console me, but I felt worse than I had at my Mother's hands in her bedroom that day. I confronted Larry about the loan and he said that he had just "pissed the money away" doing whatever he wanted. I was devastated, and felt used and foolish for working and paying all of our bills while letting him do as he pleased. I realized then that I could have just gotten away from my parents by moving, but I had gotten married in the Catholic Church; according to my upbringing, my marriage would have to last forever. Our relationship immediately became one more way in which my programming told me that I was trapped, and that all hope for a happy life was gone, because divorce was not an option.

At this time, Larry had taken a job as a truck driver and would be gone for days at a time. When he left town the following week, I packed up all my belongings and moved back into my parents' house. The following weekend, he showed up at their doorstep, once again begging me to come back to him. I told him no.

After spending several weeks at my parents' house, I started looking for an apartment. Larry even went with me on my search but I could never make the commitment to obtain an apartment. But that freedom I had felt was too good to forfeit, and I realized I could no longer fit into my parents' hierarchy and be the little girl at the bottom. One day, Larry showed up and he seemed different than usual. He was very calm this time—not needy like he had been before, when he was trying to play my emotions. He told me that I could have everything and that he would just leave me alone. I felt that he was finally showing some maturity and that made me think I could trust him again, so we began spending time together and I moved back into our mobile home. I insisted that we sell it so that I would share no financial responsibility with him, thinking that would help me feel safe in the situation.

It would be a very long time before I trusted him again, though. Right away I wondered if I had made a mistake by coming back to him. I watched his every move, waiting for him to make mistakes so I could catch him being *wrong* and blame him for my unhappiness. This is how I was taught to deal with others—if someone disappoints you, you berate them and punish them with both your words and your demeanor toward them. I began letting other men catch my attention because I told myself that I would never trust him again and that he would one day betray me with his lies. When I felt lonely, I flirted with other men to reassure myself that someday, someone else might still want me. Larry and I grew more and more distant from one another.

Without either a sense of hope or purpose in my life, I spent my days feeling vacant. I felt lost and alone, abandoned emotionally by the only person who I thought loved me. And once again, I felt trapped. I knew I couldn't spend the rest of my life this way, waking up feeling the same utter misery each and every morning.

Chapter 6

The hope that life was going to give me arrived on April 7, 1982, weighing seven pounds and twelve ounces. We named her Gina Louise. When I found myself pregnant at the age of twenty-three, I knew right away that I would name a daughter for my Mother, Louise. I thought this gesture would make her happy, but more importantly, I thought that she would finally see that I was a good daughter, for the first time in my life.

The day after Gina was born, my Mother came to see us in the hospital. The following day, she was admitted into the hospital for heart problems. She stayed in there until her death, constantly beset with new complications. Once, I received special permission from the nurses to take my baby daughter into her room; that was the second and last time my Mother ever saw her. She was buried the day before Gina's previously-scheduled baptism.

Chapter 7

I experienced a wide range of emotions when my Mother died at the age of sixty-four. At first, I was disappointed to know that I could never show her my daughter again and through Gina, gain the approval I never received as a child. I thought that becoming a mother would be something that my own mother would finally approve of, and she would finally see that I was worthy of her love. I imagined that a lifetime of suffering would disappear, as long as I could see the approval in her face. But now, the hope of being a good daughter was gone forever.

The Dream of Being

Weeks after her death, I began to experience relief. I started feeling a peace inside myself that I had never felt before—I no longer had to live up to her expectations, and her disapproval and criticism could no longer be a constant influence on my perception of myself! I felt true freedom for the first time since I was eight years old, and I realized that I was glad she was dead. For the first time, I realized that I hated her, and I hated the way she had made me feel.

My Father, however, seemed to be lost without his old life. Shortly after her death, he lost his job but was able to receive a pension from the company. My parents had been married for thirty years. Six months after my Mother passed away, my Father met and married someone from a "Parents without Partners" group and moved to Springfield, Illinois. His six adult children, their spouses and all the grandchildren were really just strangers to him; a new wife, a new home, and a new life provided a convenient escape from the aftermath of his parental choices.

With his move, my Father needed to sell his house and asked me if we would be interested in buying it through a land contract with him. We were renting a house

Chapter 7

in Erlanger, and I jumped at the chance to own something so substantial. We moved into the two year-old brick house in Burlington, Kentucky, that they had built shortly after I married. My parents had sold their old home and built a house right up the street from my older sister. In my perception, my Mother viewed her as the golden child who never could do any wrong.

Gina was nine months old when we moved into our new home, and she was a welcome diversion in my life, as I continued to shove all of the haunting thoughts and memories into the back of my mind. I was also grateful to have such a beautiful baby during the turbulent times in my marriage. Gina had a beautiful smile, and people would stop me wherever we went to tell me how beautiful she was. With light blond hair, olive skin, and dark brown eyes, one couldn't help but notice her striking good looks. She was truly a gift—a happy child and always easygoing.

Shortly after she was born, I left my career at the insurance company. Larry kept going in and out of jobs, though, and I knew that I would have to continue to provide a stable income for us. As I took on the financial responsibility for my family, I grew jealous of the bond that formed between Larry and Gina. She would run to him instead of me, clearly preferring him over me oftentimes. I was devastated once again—here was someone I loved, someone I *created*, and I thought she would be guaranteed to give me the love I so wanted. I thought she would give me the affirmation I needed to feel good about myself, but instead I felt rejected.

I felt that there was a tension between us early on, and she would push my buttons to get my attention and hurt my feelings. I felt guilty for not spending more time with her, in addition to resenting the time that Larry spent with her.

Having a child and supporting the three of us felt overwhelming. I became my Mother, giving orders and controlling every facet of our lives that I could, so everything would seem right to the programming of my mind. If I focused on keeping everything in order around me, I never had the chance to look inside myself and see the mess there.

Still, we got phone calls from bill collectors. I wasn't spending enough time with my daughter. I blamed Larry for everything, and I resented him more and more. I was

Chapter 7

determined that we would not lose our house, though, and I gave up on trying to be my daughter's favorite person.

During these years, my relations with my brothers and sisters deteriorated. I would visit my Father in Springfield and he would stay with us when he came to visit all his children and grandchildren. My Dad enjoyed staying with us because we didn't judge him for remarrying so soon, but it infuriated some of my siblings. They treated him with both disrespect and cruelty—just as our parents taught us. We had all learned our lessons well—if anyone disappoints you or breaks your rules, you punish them relentlessly.

My Father was eventually diagnosed with pancreatic cancer, and his wife, Jane, needed help with him, as she worked to support them. My siblings found it difficult to commit to helping, as they lived five hours away and we all had young children. Some of them refused to entertain the idea, since the concept of going above and beyond to help someone else was never part of our programming as children.

Larry and I would go to Illinois for weekends to spend time with my Father before he passed away. I recall lying

The Dream of Being

in the bed next to him, holding his hand and talking to him. It felt odd and uncomfortable—something akin to the wedding photo experience—but I forced myself to leave my comfort zone so I could share something meaningful with him.

One day, we were packed and ready to go up there for the weekend when I received a phone call and learned he had passed away. Funeral arrangements were made, and all of my siblings attended my Father's layout. He was laid in an open coffin for viewing and paying our final respects in the church that he and his wife attended. The next morning was his burial, and the only families who showed up were mine and one of my brother's. After the layout the previous evening, one of my sisters and a brother had said they might attend the burial. With tears streaming down my face and the hearse ready to leave the parking lot with my Father's body, I told my Father's wife that I was going to wait for the other siblings to arrive and meet them at the burial site. They never showed and I was shocked at how cold they could be toward him. I was devastated and lost it emotionally. I went home without saying goodbye to my

Father. Larry drove the whole way, trying to console me as I cried for the entire five hours.

The cruelty of my siblings that day was a perfect mirror of what I felt inside myself from how my parents had treated me. I hated all of them for what they had become, and witnessing my parents' hatefulness once again, this time directed at one of them, was more than I could stand. To protect my only child at this time and my own emotions, I distanced myself from my brothers and sisters. I couldn't fathom having to relive that kind of behavior over and over again, and most importantly, I did not want my child to be exposed to that kind of indifference to others.

* Chapter 8 *

After four years of financial instability and feeling that I needed something more to bring joy to my life, we decided to have another child. Julie Ann was born on June 12, 1986. I was bound and determined that this child would bond with me. Larry was back at his truck-driving job, but his income hardly contributed to the family finances because he always ended up with speeding tickets that required most of his salary to pay. On the Sunday morning when Julie was baptized, I told Larry to find another job or to leave the three of us behind, that I was through with the rollercoaster in my life. He knew that I was serious and quit his job the following week.

He sent in applications to reputable companies on a daily basis, and landed a job with a very large corporation. Finally, our financial picture began to change. For the first time since I met him, Larry made decent money and received incredible benefits for our whole family. I was able to scale back to a part-time job and stay home with our daughters.

Julie was also beautiful, but unlike Gina, she was a stubborn baby and child. From the day she was born, she knew what she wanted and demanded to have it. We laughed at her antics most of the time, until she would behave in extremes. It was rare to see such a small creature so obstinate and controlling. There were two males that Julie would allow to hold or touch her—her father and her grandfather, Larry's dad. If any other man came near or tried to speak to her, she would bury her face until he left. She would do this for hours, if a man was around for that long. My sister Rosemary always said that she wished our Mother could have known Julie, as she was so unique.

As the girls grew over the years, I became a modified version of my Mother. I threw myself into activities with them to avoid feeling the pain that still persisted deep inside me. I put the girls into any and every activity that I thought would interest them. I shuffled them between softball and volleyball when they were young. If the girls were busy and I had somewhere to go or something to watch, I thought I was enjoying my life, but I was not reflecting on it. Life became all about what I could do with and for them. As the girls grew older, I became more involved in their activities, particularly in coaching soccer. Being a perfectionist, I obtained several licenses so I could coach my daughters' select teams. I was a drill sergeant when it came to housework, demanding perfection in every task to compensate for the imperfections I felt so acutely within myself. I thought that if I made everything look perfect, nobody could harm me, and that they wouldn't sense my weakness. I was incapable of taking criticism from anyone because the coffer was already overflowing internally.

I wore a suit of armor at all times so no criticism could possibly threaten my fragile inner world. Early in my adult life, I realized that my appearance could be my armor. I held on tightly to whatever seemed to win the approval of others, and I consciously chose to make my appearance "perfect." I would wear the latest hairstyle, clothes, and accessories so that I always looked like I had just left the cover of a fashion magazine. Whether or not I liked it or agreed with it, I did whatever seemed to make others find me acceptable.

I had discovered that my parents, and especially my Mother, were also more approving when I tried to perfect my appearance. As a child, the majority of my play clothes were hand-me-downs from my brothers. I had a school uniform, one good church dress for Sunday, and those play clothes. At a high school basketball game once, a classmate asked me if I had any clothes other than the shirt and striped pants that I always wore to the games. That was the first time that I became self-conscious of what I wore and took notice of my appearance.

Not surprisingly, I dressed my daughters like miniature fashion models, with becoming hairstyles. Any hint of criticism toward them and I became a lioness ready to pounce on anyone who threatened her cubs. All of my concern with appearances and clothing was a whole new experience, but it was just another temporary crutch—a subconscious diversion to keep my conscious mind from acknowledging the hell that lay beneath my suit of armor.

I knew that I wasn't happy, and I grasped onto anything I could to help me find the elusive peace I longed for. That is, I grasped onto anything outside myself.

My typical day was planned to the minute, utilizing all of my many programmed tactics to help me navigate through the tasks I created for myself. The first order of the day was to rise at 6:30 in the morning, shower, get dressed, and lay out a set of clothes to change into later, during my two-minute return home from work. On game days, I spent the thirty-minute drive to work and the ten-minute parking space search trying to come up with an excuse to give my boss so I could leave work early and get to the 6:00 soccer game on time. I needed to leave early so I could break the speed limit the whole way home and run up the stairs to my bedroom, ordering the girls to remember everything we needed while clothes were being unbuttoned, unzipped, shed, and thrown into the laundry as I passed the hamper in the hallway. If you were playing "Mother May I," it was three gigantic steps to get to my bed, where the prearranged clothes lay.

I would dress in record time, shoes and socks in hand, still barking orders to anyone who was straggling behind and rushing whichever daughter was playing to the car, along with her friends and all the necessary soccer equipment. I'd start the car with half the equipment still unsettled, demanding that they not spill their water or sports drinks, and off we headed toward the expressway and the soccer field.

Socks and shoes went on at stoplights, and when we finally arrived at the field, I dropped the girls off so they could run to their team and I went to find a parking space. I'd grab my chair and make it to the other side of the field with not a minute to spare. Then it was warm-ups, the game, a brilliant half-time speech, and dash back to the car to discuss the game and the players all the way home, with only one interruption for fast food that we ate in the car.

By the time we reached our destination—"home"—dusk had turned to darkness. Work and soccer clothes had to be washed for the next day, telephone calls from friends or acquaintances were returned, and when I finally closed my eyes, I found that I couldn't sleep for all the gremlins from the day's activities running through my mind. When they finally settled down, anxiety about the future came, and I was haunted by thoughts of being stuck in my same patterns forever, with my hopelessness and my exhausting habits. Then my inner dialogue turned to the next day's agenda. Somewhere between 1:00 and 2:00 a.m., I would finally drift to a place where nothing really mattered.

Years went by, and I just went through the motions. I was highly critical of almost everything that came to my attention, and I had no hope for a happy life, so I was bent on destroying the one I had. I was in a rut and nothing changed the way I felt inside—it didn't matter how many teams I coached at the same time, or how hard I pushed myself. I couldn't look inside myself for the pain that I was feeling, so I focused on Larry instead.

At that time, I believed that personal happiness came from other people and the things a person could have in life. One Christmas Eve, we opened our gifts and I found that Larry had given me a green warm-up suit to match the team's colors. Despite the thought he had put into it, my immediate reaction was that the color looked ugly and that he had screwed up again.

We started arguing about it, and as the fighting escalated, I went upstairs so that the children wouldn't see it. Larry followed me, insisting that I was never happy with anything. In turn, I blamed him for not having better judgment. In reality, our feelings had nothing to do with the warm-up suit—we were expressing the pain that was deep inside each of us from childhood; the situation just served as a trigger.

As our fighting intensified, Larry rushed toward me and slammed me down on the bed, grabbing my throat to choke me. I kneed him and screamed at him to get out of my life, that I hated him. He immediately went downstairs and told our daughters that we were getting divorced, hoping to gain their sympathy. Outraged that he would do that during Christmas, I was sure that I wanted him out of my life and that he had mentally damaged our girls. I was so scared that they would feel what I felt inside, and I had promised myself that they would never feel such pain. I lay there on our bed, crying and thinking of ways to kill myself.

Days went by and I felt trapped once again, not knowing how I could support my children by myself and give them the same level of material comfort. Larry and I had built a new two-story home and I couldn't imagine starting over by myself. Once again, he and I just coexisted.

Many nights, I would lie beside him in bed trying to decide whether or not to kill myself. As always, I blamed him for my pain. I couldn't truly look inside myself—that was too frightening. During these years, Larry was gruff and always negative. Cutting remarks and criticism rolled off his tongue toward anyone and everyone. We merely tolerated each other and it is clear now that I knew I did not love him then.

As my daughters grew older, I felt my control over them slipping away. I couldn't maintain the charade of making everything perfect any more, and I panicked, sensing that if I lost that illusion, I would have to face the wounded child inside me. I knew that my children's need for freedom would win out over my need for control, but I wouldn't give up without a fight. I wasn't ready to turn my attention to the lost and hurting child within who so desperately needed and deserved unconditional love.

My inner turmoil grew as I watched Gina become more and more of her own person—her own person was someone who wanted to get as far away from me and our home as possible. Because of her physical and mental maturity, older boys wanted to date Gina in middle school. Larry and I wanted to give her guidelines with more lenient rules than we each had growing up. Once she began dating, she distanced herself from our family and became secretive about her life.

Whenever we tried to communicate with her, she would say as little as possible to try to end the conversation. She was uncooperative and made it clear that she did not want to be part of our family any more. She went to the same church as whichever boy she was dating at the time, and became close to her boyfriends' mothers, going shopping with them and spending time with them. She avoided our family functions and stayed away as much as she could. Even though she would clearly be devastated when one of the relationships ended, she would never talk about it with us.

Gina thought that I liked Julie more than I liked her because I spent more time with Julie. I did not love her more, but Julie was receptive to me and would interact with me, while Gina seemed to disapprove of everything I did. It seemed that everything I did was wrong in her eyes.

Once again, I took Gina's behavior as proof that I wasn't good enough, and that Larry and I had made terrible mistakes in raising her. Her aloofness hurt deeply, and I took it all very personally. There were numerous times that I went to her room, begging her to tell me why she hated me. She would say nothing, but her whole being was telling me, "I can't stand you."

After graduating from high school, Gina went to Cincinnati State to get her degree in Horticulture. She started dating a young man named Billy and began going to his church, as she had done with her boyfriends as a teenager. The first time I met Billy, I thought he was very handsome. At this time, Julie was getting ready to be confirmed in the Catholic Church, as I still held onto my religious beliefs. Julie asked Gina to be her sponsor, but Gina refused because she said that she was becoming a Baptist.

Larry and I had no idea that she had planned to convert, but we attended Billy's church on the day Gina was baptized. When I sat down on the pew, I started feeling sick to my stomach. Billy's mother came over and offered to take pictures of Gina for us and at that point, I started crying. I felt that I had completely lost Gina, that she had chosen a new family for herself and that I was completely replaced. I got up and left the church feeling angry.

Larry came outside with me, and we left instead of staying for the baptism. It hurt Gina that we left, but I could not stay and watch her do something that I did not think was her true heart's desire. I did not think she was converting because of her spiritual beliefs, but because of her desire to be accepted by Billy and his family.

They dated for some time longer but at one point, Billy decided to call it off. Gina ended up dating a young man who lived down the street from us, someone Larry and I liked a lot. We grew closer to Gina at this time because she would bring her boyfriend to our house. Eventually, she and Billy realized that they were in love with each other and got back together. One evening, she and Billy came to the house to tell us they were engaged and going to be married. Larry and I both cried and congratulated them, and I hugged them both.

They told us this news in February, and Gina said that she wanted the wedding to take place in six months. Larry and I helped make arrangements and got everything planned within a few weeks so she could have her wedding in August as she wished. I think she was surprised at how accepting we were and how we helped her. I got the sense that she thought we would resist her plans or fight against them, but I am not sure why she would have expected that.

A few weeks before the wedding, I thought to ask Gina if Larry and I would be asked who "gives Gina away." We were not willing to say that we gave her away, as we do not believe in regarding anyone, including our children, as our property. Gina got very upset and could not understand why we would not say it for the sake of the ceremony, but the preacher talked to her and they changed the question to, "Who supports these two?" Larry and I were happy to answer, "We do" to that question. Gina had a beautiful outdoor wedding and arrived to the ceremony with her bridal party in a horse-drawn carriage.

Over the next few years, Gina and I grew to know each other as we never had before. One night, I picked her up to go to a store. As soon as she got in the car, she blurted out, "I'm pregnant." During her pregnancy, she called me whenever she had morning sickness and pains, which was frequently. I would do my holistic healing services for her and she appreciated the relief and help I provided her.

William was born on August 11, 2008, a date that I found special because 11 and 22, my birth day, are birth dates of masters. William has been a gift not only to Gina and Billy, but to Larry and me as well. Gina and I have grown much closer as we now share so much in common as mothers. I watch William for her three days a week, and having him in our lives has allowed me to get to know Gina as I never had before. I have found that Gina is a lot like Larry; she is a beautiful woman who says what she means and does not mince words.

Looking back, I see that my early experiences with Gina helped propel me into the state that I had to get to before I would abandon my attempts to control everything. I tried to control her as a child, just as my Mother had done to me. When I saw that I had failed to hold on to my control—to make her love me unquestioningly—my sense of self was shattered.

I realized that while I was asking Gina for answers, the little girl inside me wanted to ask those questions of my Mother—I was just using Gina as the vehicle for my need. I wanted to understand why it was that I was so disgusting, why she couldn't love me. I knew that I had treated Gina like my Mother had treated me, and before I truly loved and accepted myself, I felt that I deserved Gina's rejection. I cried many days and nights because I felt like such a failure. I had vowed that my children would never feel about themselves as my Mother made me feel about myself. I told myself that I didn't protect them from the monster who lived inside me—my Mother. Using her disapproving looks, words, and behavior, I had become my Mother, criticizing Gina's grades, her clothes, and how she appeared (in my mind) to the world.

With that realization, I sank further into depression, wracked with guilt. I told myself that once again, someone I loved was rejecting me and did not want me in their life because I was not good enough.

The Dream of Being

I spiraled down further and further, overwhelmed by the sense of emptiness, repulsion, disgust, and loneliness that would fill me for days. Once again, and for the last time, the child within me stepped forward and asked to be acknowledged. In my usual way, I turned to the diversion tactics I had used for so long, but I found that I was too exhausted from running for so long. I finally surrendered, and allowed her to be heard.

Chapter 9

Healing from the Other Side

I was working at Toyota in Erlanger, Kentucky, in the early months of 2001 when my sister Rosemary told me that she had some information to share with me. She explained that she and our brother David went somewhere over the weekend and that our paternal grandmother from *the other side* had communicated with him, telling him that I had been sexually molested.

David had undergone open heart surgery as a child and had an out-of-body experience during the operation. He saw our parents in the waiting room while he was

The Dream of Being

being operated on, and he passed into the other side during the procedure. Afterwards, he was able to see and hear spirits. As an adult, he told me that he had asked our Mother about the spirits, and she told him not to mention it to anyone.

While walking down a hallway with me at one of the Toyota headquarters, Rosemary explained what had transpired over the weekend. My brothers and sisters never knew what had happened to me when I was eight, and as she described the details, I walked silently and felt stiffness overtake my body. I told her that I was fine and that it didn't matter, to which she responded that it was obvious I wasn't fine—tears were welling up in my eyes and I needed to talk about it. When I told her what had happened, her mouth dropped open and she expressed her shock—she had had no idea.

After a couple of days passed and the significance of this intervention from the other side sank in, I called my brother. I was intrigued and amazed by the communication he recounted with our grandmother, and he also told me that one of my guides on the other side told him that I should read *Conversations with God* by Neale Donald

Chapter 9

Walsch. I knew that there was no other logical explanation for how David could have gotten the information about what had happened to me, so I bought Book One of Walsch's trilogy and began reading.

I would sit in the living room and read as Larry watched television, interrupting his viewing by reading sentences or words that resonated with me. With tears in my eyes, I looked at him and told him one night that I never did anything wrong as a child. I realized that I am not a bad person, and I am not damned. I knew that the words I read in that book were *truth*—God's truth—especially for me.

After reading the first book, I read everything else that Walsch wrote. I began meditating and trying to listen to my spirit guides. I started writing in a journal and took note of anything new and different in my life. It was amazing how fast my life changed when I said *YES* to it. As I worked on changing my thoughts and my behaviors, I experienced life from a new view, with a completely different attitude.

The experience with Rosemary and David was divine intervention, and the turning point in my life. I had to surrender what I thought I knew, and I began to see how exhausting it was to hold onto my illusions and all of my negativity.

As I shut down my old thoughts and ideas from my programmed mind, doors opened and I discovered new possibilities that the hell of my imagination could never perceive. The very first thing that I knew I had to do was to stop the negative chatter that consumed my life. I taught myself how to meditate, and I used every free moment to shut down the ticker-tape of my mind. My programming became less powerful as I gave it less of my energy, and after three months, I could obtain the state of nothingness in my mind.

When I reached that state, I looked forward to meditating every chance I got. At first, it was so exciting just to be with me, my spirit, and not hear a thing. I cherished this time and could stay in the state of nothingness for over an hour. It was not long after I achieved this treasured state that I began to receive messages that gave me insight into my life and the lives of others. I still remember those initial revelations, and how exciting it was to be trusted by the divine spirits with such information, with the gift of *knowingness*.

People ask if I hear a voice, and how I *know* that what I'm hearing is true. It is a state that I cannot explain, but I trust that it is truth without a doubt because there is no logic or thinking involved. The information flows freely, without any ego-serving messages. In addition to meditating, I also learned during that same year how to use rods and dowsing to confirm the messages I received. It blew my mind that this was possible!

My world did not stop expanding, and it made another amazing shift in 2002, when I began to see energy. While reading one night, I noticed a fine haze around my legs. I stared at it for hours, amazed at what I saw, which was the first energy layer around every person's body. From then on, I would stare past everyone I encountered, wanting to see if I could perceive their energy. It was so fun to do this, especially during meetings at work, when I would occupy myself by examining different parts of a person's auric field.

During this year, I learned about using pendulums and took hands-on healing classes—Reiki I and II. Diane, the instructor for those classes, told me that I was going to go far in regard to energy work. In addition, I began socializing and meeting with two people who could communicate with spirits from the other side—one of those people was my brother David, who had helped in my divine intervention. The communication from the other side always fascinated me, and I loved hearing what my parents said and being able to communicate with them.

I also started a spiritual study group discussing the *Conversations with God* books. I was always putting groups together in my spare time to have psychic parties and to study spirituality. I was on a fast-track and moving so fast that I felt pulled back by an energy that did not want me to move so quickly. My journal entry from September 2, 2002 reads: "This is a confusing time for me right now. I feel as though I am not progressing or going forward. I need a boost from one of my spirit guides or angels to give me direction. I feel lost right now and don't know what to do. I would love to know where my future lies and its direction. Please help me/guide me. I don't know what to do."

Chapter 9

I didn't write in my journal again until October 2002; this is what I wrote: "It was a Saturday evening in October and I was at my brother's house and had to leave. I looked at the clock and it was 10:10 p.m. and at that moment I heard in my ear from a source connected to the universe that my youngest daughter, Julie, would see a boy by the name of Jason that evening." (This was not a person that I felt she was safe with.)

"I picked her up the next morning and she said that she saw Jason at 10:10 p.m. because she looked at the car clock. I didn't mention to her until after then that it was the exact time that I had remembered seeing at my brother's house." This was the beginning of my realization that my life would never be the same again. Life and events started becoming very synchronistic.

In 2003, my spiritual journey took a turn that would change my life forever. Since the *Conversations with God* books had such a profound impact on me, I began reading Neale Donald Walsch's website. I was searching for direction, since I realized that my old programming no longer served me. I saw online that a special event would be taking place—Humanity's Team Conference in

Portland, Oregon, sponsored by the Conversations with God Foundation, and the first of its kind.

It took a lot of courage for me to tell my husband that I wanted to attend the conference—I was not programmed to do anything that the people around me were not doing or were not receptive to. I approached Larry and told him that I wanted to attend so I could see what it was all about; I also told him that I wanted him to travel with me. Being the wonderful, open-minded person he is, Larry agreed to go.

We traveled to Portland and I found that being with positive individuals daily who are on a high level of consciousness was one of the most incredible feelings in my life. The speakers and the entertainers resonated with both of us in ways that we had never experienced in all our years dealing with organized religion, and the shared experience brought us closer to each other. The speakers talked about having the freedom to find one's own path and trusting one's spirit. Most importantly, they said that no matter what a person did, God still loved them.

I learned of a Leadership Education Program that taught how to understand the spiritual principals of

Conversations with God and to share them with groups. I did not think I could join the program because of the expense, and my programming still told me that I was not intelligent enough to participate and that I was limited by a shortage of money. One day, while meditating in my living room, I asked for guidance in regard to the classes. From my limited perspective, they seemed expensive and as if they would require too much of my time.

The answer I received scared the hell out of me—literally. My body shook and I heard a booming voice say, "You will do this." I jumped up from the recliner I was sitting in and looked around—the voice sounded as if it was coming from someone next to me. I had never experienced anything like it before, and without hesitation, I ran upstairs to my computer and signed up for the program.

The program lasted for two years and involved interaction with Neale Donald Walsch and other coaches, who were all such gifted individuals. Flying to Oregon was a requirement, as well as attending a retreat at which we discussed the contents of Walsch's books and questions that arose as the retreat unfolded. It was an exhausting but infinitely rewarding experience that I would never trade for anything.

During this entire educational process, I compared myself to others and felt so inadequate. However, I had completed the Life Coaching program and when I returned from the retreat, I offered those services to the handful of clients who came to see me at my home for Reiki treatments. The combination of Life Coaching, based on spiritual principles, and Reiki accelerated the healing process of individuals' bodies and minds. It was incredibly powerful, though difficult for people to accept if they were not open to new ways of thinking.

It wasn't always easy, exploring all of these new ideas and new ways of thinking that were foreign to my family. The first time I tried to describe Reiki to my husband and daughters, their eyes glazed over in response. Some people commented that I had gone crazy, and others suggested that I was involved with a cult. The fact that I heard things from the other side about their own lives was mind-blowing to them. I once overheard my future son-in-law chastising Gina about this way of life that I had introduced to all of them, and her belief in all the unbelievable information.

But even when there was no external support for my journey, I knew that everything I was experiencing was real and legitimate; I knew the possibilities were endless. I would not let anyone's judgment, criticism, or incredulity keep me from exploring my newfound world. I had finally discovered freedom, and I would not return to the hellhole of my mind just to keep everyone else comfortable. Everything I was doing and talking about defied the rules of what seemed possible to those around me, and stepping beyond that always rouses fear in people who feel safe in being constricted and controlled by their own programming. At one time, I was that way, too—but I was changing.

Another miraculous event occurred in October 2002, and is one which I will never forget. My journal entry reads: "For the three previous months, I have really struggled with my emotions about everything changing in my life. One early Sunday morning in October, I rolled over in bed and there before my eyes was my Mother who had passed away. She materialized in front of me in her pink and white dress that she wore to my wedding. My immediate reaction was to put my arms around her and kiss her on the cheek. She then disappeared."

Years later, I understand that this event marked the turning point in my life when I stopped hating my Mother, and began to understand the meaning of the drama between us, especially in my childhood. I also realized that I had grown strong enough to allow her to assist me on my spiritual journey—to help me heal further so I could keep moving forward. From that remarkable morning forward, I have used my Mother as a spiritual guide in my life and she is the first spiritual being I turn to when I need an answer.

As I grew more confident in my new direction, I made a life-altering decision that shattered some of the most stubborn programming from my youth. I had always been taught that I would graduate from high school and obtain a job immediately. I was not expected to go to college, so I did not think of it as an option. From the age of eighteen to forty-six, I sought job security by working for large corporations. I was programmed to think that as long as I worked from 8 a.m. to 5 p.m. every day and gave 110%, I would be safe in this world.

In 1997, I had begun to sense a conflict inside me that was increasing in strength. I realized that I resented working like I had been, and I questioned whether I could continue doing it for the rest of my life. The answer, I knew, was a resounding *no*.

By July 2004, I was ready to make a new start. I rocked my family's world—and my own—by leaving my position at a well-established corporation to open a holistic business. At first, I was nervous and scared to approach Larry with my idea, considering the insecurities he had about money and the problems it had caused our marriage in the past. To my surprise, the part of him that I love most responded to me. With his unconditional love and open mind, he told me to do what made me happy, and that we would somehow make it work.

As the last day at my job drew near, I felt even more nervous and began to worry and scare myself, asking how I would ever make this work and find enough clients to support my business. I planned to call it "Reiki of Northern Kentucky," but at that time, very few people in

Northern Kentucky knew what Reiki was—how would they know that they needed my services?

Because of my doubt, I thought it would be best to invest as little money as possible in the business to start. I planned to work out of my home, but the force that was orchestrating my life did not agree with that decision.

One day, while I was still in my corporate position, I received a phone call from a woman seeking Reiki. She came to my house and we had the session; a couple of days later, she called me for another treatment. I was still at the office when I heard her message, and she asked me to come by her house because she had been drinking alcohol and did not want to drive. I was so excited to have a new client—it seemed that my business was going to increase, after all. But I was still in "Mother Theresa" mode, so eager to help people that I went along with her request without careful consideration.

I called the woman back and got directions to her home. During the entire forty-minute drive to her house, my inner voice kept saying, "Don't go!" I was stubborn, though, and chose to ignore it. When she opened the door, I found myself facing a glassy-eyed woman who seemed full of wildness inside herself. I entered her home and she proceeded to show me every picture she had hanging on her walls, touching each of them gingerly as if she would never see them again.

While she went through the house in this manner, clearly displaying a deep level of pain, she explained that her phone was dead and that a repairman was on his way to fix it. She eventually sat on the couch and I joined her, trying to offer consolation as she wept. Ten minutes later, the doorbell rang and her tears disappeared, as if a faucet had been turned off. She opened the door and spoke with the repairman, who said he would go behind the house to check the phone connection.

She closed the front door and then walked down a hallway and disappeared into a room. A few minutes passed and I heard some noises from where she had gone, and I called her name. I felt that something was wrong and I walked toward the noise. When I reached the doorway, I found her loading a handgun. My body froze and I told myself over and over, "Remain calm." I asked her to please put the gun down, and with a look of despair on her face, she told me there was no use in living.

The Dream of Being

    I immediately called upon my Mother on the other side to protect and help me in this situation, so everyone could have the best outcome. It was not a second later that the doorbell rang in the living room. I knew that this moment was my opportunity to change the situation. Frozen by the sound of the doorbell, she stopped what she was doing. I grabbed the gun and ran to the door, pushing past the repairman. I could hear her chasing me, then suddenly stopping to talk to him as if nothing was wrong. Several years later, that beautiful lady committed suicide while someone was in her living room.

    After that incident, I realized that if I was going to help people, it had to be away from my family's home, their safe haven. I immediately began looking for an office space once I had this realization. I was scouring ads and asking everyone I knew about available spaces, when Larry suggested an area close to the interstate exit in Erlanger. He drove me to the area, and there were several signs for office space within different buildings. I called multiple numbers and only one person called me back—and it happened to be for the building that was on the corner and easiest to find for anyone not familiar with the area.

I made an appointment to look at the space right away, and of course it was perfect. The building was a former bed and breakfast that had been converted to small offices. Entering the front door feels like coming into a home; the dining room on the right is a conference room and there is a kitchen to the left, through a swinging door. Best of all, the lease was reasonable and the manager told me that I could pay in any arrangement I wanted. No longer did I have fears of a long lease agreement and expensive financial commitments.

I accepted the space, but the universe was not through with me yet. One of the dearest angels in my life approached me the following day and told me about a doctor's office that was closing. I contacted the doctor to see what she had for sale, and was able to furnish my office with everything I needed for $180.

Every objection that my old programming had conjured was removed—a force bigger than myself was directing my life.

Still, my old programming reared its ugly head again. With a week left at my corporate job, I was faced with new obstacles. I started asking myself how I could possibly contribute to my household by taking this route. I wanted a way out of the craziness that I suddenly felt I was in, and I wanted to hold onto the security blanket that my old job provided me.

I was no longer excited about the unknown, but scared. I challenged the higher force that had taken over my life—while sitting at my desk one day during that last week, I looked up at the ceiling in desperation and thought, "If you want me to do this, then there better be a message on my business phone by the time I return from lunch."

A business line had just been installed at my new office the day before, and only a handful of people knew about my services. I told myself that this was the impossible—my rational mind knew that the Universe could not possibly deliver on this ultimatum, and that I would go back to my safe little cocoon, trudging along in my ordinary existence.

Chapter 9

I grabbed my purse and went home for lunch. During that hour, I told myself that all of the new revelations and abilities of the past two years had been a dream, and that it would soon be over. Whatever had compelled me to do what I had done and to make such crazy decisions—well, that was going to leave me alone, once and for all.

I returned from lunch and cautiously eyed the phone that sat on my desk, knowing there would be no message in the voicemail for my brand-new business. I picked up the receiver and dialed the number for message retrieval, closing my eyes and waiting to hear the female computer voice say, "There are no new messages."

I almost dropped the phone when, instead, the automated voice told me, "You have one new message." It was a woman who was requesting information about my services and who wished to set up an appointment. I placed the phone down with deliberate reverence, collapsed into my chair, and let the tears stream from my eyes.

I don't know how long I sat there, dazed by the sanctity of that moment I had just experienced. I finally knew that the powers guiding me to this unexplored territory were not letting me run away, no matter what kind of excuses I tried to make. I was walking to the edge of a cliff, but I knew I would fly—and I left corporate America.

Chapter 10

After leaving my job, I spent the first two days working on my new business space, preparing it so it would reflect the sacred work I was now turning my energy toward. Friends offered to help me, but I knew that I had to paint it and arrange the furniture myself, with help only from my husband. My energy had to be the only energy in the room, so it would attract the clients who needed the services I offered at that time: Reiki and life-coaching.

I contacted the local library and a support group, offering to give presentations about my services. With those contacts and a small clientele, my business took off.

I gave all of myself to every individual who scheduled an appointment. After a single session with one person, I usually had one or two phone calls from friends and relatives, wanting to get information or to make an appointment for themselves. I kept telling myself to just focus on the person, and everything would fall into place.

I did have clients, however, who did not seem to be changed or helped after a session, leaving me feeling inadequate and as if I had failed. I sought out more healing knowledge so I would have answers. I added new modalities to my work, obtaining certifications in EFT (Emotional Freedom Technique) and Hypnotherapy, and became a Board-Certified Holistic Health Counselor and Practitioner. In no time at all, I had 200 clients and gained more constantly, with my only advertising being word-of-mouth.

Even though I had learned so much while studying with Neale Donald Walsch and the Conversations with God Foundation, I still felt as though there was so much more to learn and I wanted to be more challenged spiritually. Through a fellow student at the Foundation, I was made aware of the Beloved Community, founded by

James Twyman, spiritual author, singer and producer. James has a dedication to St. Francis and his community's philosophy is based on this great saint. When I became a Reiki Master several years earlier, St. Francis came to me in a meditation and said that he would be my healing guide.

When I discovered the Beloved Community, I did not know that St. Francis's teachings were their basis. While researching The Beloved Community and James Twyman, I realized that St. Francis was leading me in this direction. I studied with The Beloved Community in the Seminary program and obtained even greater discoveries about who I was, hidden religious information and energies that are held sacred throughout the world. On June 11, 2006, I was ordained by James Twyman as a Peace Minister in Medford, Oregon at a beautiful spiritual retreat in the mountains. It is a day that I will never forget!

The more I worked with people, the stronger my intuition became. People would look at me in wonder, asking how I knew things about them as we spoke about their issues. At first, I did not always realize what I was

The Dream of Being

saying or where the information was coming from. It hit me one day that I was listening to people's thoughts and experiences, without them saying a word.

Intrigued by this development, I realized that I was hearing people's energy fields and I began to research that phenomenon. I found that all of a person's thoughts and experiences reside in their energy fields around their body. Fascinated, I decided to play with the concept and see how it could be used in other ways.

I had seen my brother and one other medium provide flame card readings for people. I decided to try it for myself, incorporating my ability to hear a person's energy field. I offered to do them for friends and "for fun" at the end of the classes I had begun teaching, classes like "Who Am I?" and "Feel & See Energy." People enjoyed the information from the flame card readings and what I saw so much that I began offering them on a weekly basis for a nominal fee.

At first, I was afraid that I would tell someone incorrect information about their future, that I would be wrong. But the more I played with the readings, the more comfortable I became, and the more comfortable I became, the more accurate the information was. If I knew I was going to be doing card flame readings for a group, I would stay awake the night before, afraid that no information would come to me. I would beg the Universe and my spirit guides to be with me and to help me. They never let me down. The only impediment I ever experienced was my own fear, which kept me from hearing the information.

In a flame card reading, one writes their name on an index card and I hold the card over a candle flame. The person's spirit guides control the way the flame singes the card and use it to create images of people, spirits or special objects in that person's life. Since I can also hear the energy of the person getting the reading, and voices from the other side, I receive a lot of messages as to what someone's current concerns are, what is unhealed inside them and what future situations are unfolding for them.

When a spirit tells me what image is on the card, and I tell the client about the special object or person being described to me, almost every client begins to cry, knowing that I am truly connecting with something special in their lives. I can give details and accounts of situations that only the receiver of the reading would know, and that ensures people that they're not getting vague information that could apply to anyone.

In July of 2009, I went to a workshop led by the renowned Medium, James Van Praagh. I planned to let that experience decide whether I would continue providing medium services to others, or if I would stop. I wanted to know if I was good at what I was doing, or if I should focus my energy elsewhere. During the workshop, I did readings on a stage for the first time and in front of a large audience for the first time. The results were all positive, and I continue to receive phone calls from people across the United States who were there, requesting readings from me. This experience gave me a lot of confidence in my ability, and I began conducting group spirit message forums in hotel conference rooms, which has been a great success and is still growing.

Providing this kind of service for others can be daunting—sometimes, people decide to base very important decisions on what I tell them. One evening in 2010, my phone rang and I did not recognize the number, so I did not answer it. I checked my email before going to bed and saw that someone wanted to add me as a friend on a social networking website; I did not recognize her, so I ignored the request. Then, I read my email and she had emailed me again, saying that I had done a reading for her nine months earlier and that all the explanation I needed was in her "friend" request, so I went back and accepted it. She called me the next day.

During our first reading, I had told her that she would be pregnant within the year, and she was. She wanted to know who the father was—her boyfriend, or someone else. I heard that the baby was her boyfriend's, and that it was the one with the reddish tint in his hair. She said that was her boyfriend, and asked if it was the one who has children or not. I heard that he did have children, and she said it could not be him, because her boyfriend did not have children. However, the spirit said that he did have a child, whether he knew it or not, and I told her this as well.

Just then, the woman's grandmother interjected and said that she should not listen to a blond person, and she should not do what the blond says. When I told her this, the woman yelled into the phone that she was standing next to her blond-haired friend—they were at an abortion clinic, and the blond woman was trying to convince her to have an abortion. She said that she had to go, and hung up the phone. I emailed her later to ask what happened, and the woman wrote me back and said that she decided to keep the baby. She had planned to make her decision to keep the baby or have an abortion based on whatever I told her over the phone.

This experience scared the hell out of me. I did not want to live other people's lives for them, and I made myself sick for the next two weeks. I told Larry that I was not going to provide medium services for people anymore—I was afraid of giving people wrong information and of people making such big decisions based on what I said. But Larry, my knight in shining armor, told me that I had just saved a baby's life, and asked how I could think that was a bad thing. That encouraged me to keep doing this work, and to trust the spirits to guide me.

My work with spirit communication led to another incredible day when I was driving to work about a week before Easter the same year. As I got close to the interstate exit I take to my office, I saw an SUV with a trailer pulled over on the side of the busy road. One man was at the vehicle and another walked ahead, toward the exit ramp. I heard a female voice clearly say, "Stop," so I pulled over and asked the man if he needed help. He said that he did, he needed to get gas for his vehicle.

The interstate sign said that there was a gas station two-tenths of a mile off the exit, but I knew there was not a gas station that close. I drove him to the nearest one and we got the gas. As we drove, he asked me why I picked him up. I replied that I did not know if he believed in this sort of thing or not, but that I am a Medium and a psychic, and I was told that he was safe to pick up. He said that he wished more people believed in that sort of thing, and showed me pictures of his children and family. He thanked me when I dropped him off near his vehicle, and I went on my way to my office.

That morning, I did two readings. One man drove an hour and a half for his appointment and when we started, I said that he had a son. His eyes teared up, and then I said that he was in trouble with the court system and he started crying. His grandfather was communicating with me, and told me that the man had been abused. The man said he had not.

The Dream of Being

Then, his grandfather said he was thinking of taking his son and running off with him, and that he should not do it. His grandfather also said that if he did, he would never see his son again and it would ruin his life. The man was astounded, and I was told again that he was beaten as a child. I said to him, "Your father beat you." This time, he replied, "Yeah, he did beat me pretty good."

Then, I heard from a friend of his on the other side, and I identified the friend by his first name. At that point, he kind of lost it—he could not believe what I was telling him and all that I knew. Our session ended and he walked out into the hallway, where he stood for a moment, as if he was trying to collect himself. His grandfather told me to hug him, so I went out and asked him if I could. He let me hug him and started crying in my arms.

Another thing that had come out during the reading was that he had hit his wife and children—he had a lot of anger inside of him, and a lot of monsters to deal with. I told him that he could use EFT to help address his anger, and that he could look at the website to get more information about that. That was a powerful and magical day, and I think that my work really changed his life.

* Chapter 11 *

After seeing my Mother as a spirit in my room, my behavior toward the rest of my family began to change. At family functions, I had always felt uncomfortable and unwelcome. I dreaded going and cried afterwards—I could not understand why my family, this group of people that was supposed to love each other, was so mean and hurtful toward one another.

I have always been over-sensitive to criticism, and I came to realize that I felt that way because I had always felt like a disappointment to my parents, and particularly to my Mother. But our entire family fostered negative relationships and critical attitudes as well. Every night when I was a child, whoever sat at the kitchen table had a free-for-all verbal battle. Our only goal was to hurt, ridicule, and demean one another; we succeeded if we managed to hurt someone's feelings or make them angry. One night, one of my sisters grew so angry she began pulling wall decorations down and throwing them.

We were always fighting, hitting and yelling at each other. We were brought up to trounce on one another and keep each other down. When I began my spiritual journey, I decided I did not want to treat people like that. I wanted to hug them, to let them know that they were not a threat to me, and I believe that my decision to do so helped my family begin to hug one another.

On Thanksgiving of 2002, Larry, my daughters and I went to Rosemary's house. When I arrived, and for the first time ever, I deliberately hugged every family member, determined to be a positive presence.

The following Saturday, I did Reiki on Rosemary and her daughter Laura at my house. It was a very spiritual experience for the three of us. While I was working on Rosemary, Laura said that she could see green and purple energy all around her mother, and she was overwhelmed with emotion at her ability to see it.

When I placed my hands over Rosemary's heart, I began to cry, sensing the depth of heartache and pain she held inside. During our session, I noticed that she had a lot of negative energy in her pelvic area, and I suggested that she go see a gynecologist. She dismissed what I said, but in February 2003, she was diagnosed with ovarian cancer.

I wanted to help my sister, but I also realized that it is fruitless to want for or try to change someone else's spiritual journey and outcome. Rosemary was told that she had a mass over her cervix. When I found out, I went to her house for several days during my lunch hour so I could do Reiki on her. My hands felt sticky and moist whenever I pulled them away from her pelvic area, and I realized that I was feeling the cancer inside her.

During that same month—February of 2003—I took Rosemary and Laura to my Reiki Master, from whom I received Reiki Master certification. Maureen and I worked on Rosemary for over two and a half hours. Maureen said that the cancer was also on Rosemary's kidney, and we could see Rosemary's stomach visibly deflating, as it was swelled due to the cancer. Maureen pulled me aside and told me that she could feel the fear inside Rosemary, though she claimed to feel good when we left.

On February 24, 2003, Rosemary underwent an operation at 11:30 in the morning. She received a complete hysterectomy, and the doctors found that the cancer was recycling through her bowels. On February 28, my Mother came to me and told me that Rosemary would not survive. For the next four years, she battled cancer with chemotherapy and radiation treatments.

During 2006, Rosemary became distant with me and put up walls between us whenever I saw her. It was difficult to accept and understand, especially when there had been no drama between us. I tried to tell her in different ways that I loved her. She continually rejected my attempts, but my Mother reassured me that I should try to understand and have compassion for Rosemary.

I gained interesting insights during the last few weeks of Rosemary's life. On Christmas of 2006, all of my siblings and I gathered at our oldest sister's house. Rosemary was brought into the living room and laid on the couch. Everyone was sad because we knew that it would be the last time that we were all together in this lifetime.

Even though Rosemary was not speaking to me, I went over to her, hugged her, and whispered in her ear, "I'm sorry that I did anything to hurt you." She responded, "It doesn't matter anymore." I kissed her and told her that I loved her.

The next day, I grew angry, feeling I had betrayed myself by apologizing to her. To be honest, I was not sorry for anything—I had come to understand that we are all doing our best at all times, coping with the demons and programming in our minds. Anything that we say or do is a reflection of how we feel about ourselves.

But there had been no cross words or unkind transgressions between Rosemary and me. She created her resentment and anger out of a need to judge me as harshly as she was judging herself. The anger within me subsided once I recognized that I had betrayed myself in an attempt to give someone else a chance to use my words to find peace within herself. Rosemary's battle with cancer ended on January 4, 2007.

The day she was to be laid out at the funeral home, I awoke with an intestinal virus. I realized that my body was releasing toxins that were associated with my relationship with my sister. I had allowed her to have emotional control over me, and once that control was gone, all of the negativity associated with it was suddenly being let go. I welcomed that healing.

At the funeral, my husband was the only male member of our family who was not asked to be a pallbearer. Once again, my family was acting out their programming that we learned from our parents—punish anyone who disappoints or displeases you. Larry and I were not offended, as we had both outgrown that level of delusional programming, that effort to project negativity toward others. The old me—what I call Version One—would have been crushed, telling herself yet again that her family never loved or wanted her.

In challenging times, it is absolutely wonderful to realize how much one has grown and healed, but even more amazing to feel self-love. At Rosemary's funeral, I realized that as long as I knew who I was and loved myself, no one could hurt me.

Regardless of the lies that Rosemary had told her family and my siblings about me, I knew who I was and I wanted to exude the love that existed inside me toward everyone at the funeral. I was no longer mentally wounded—I was strong and had clarity. I was not sad that my sister passed on because of the reassurance I got from conversations that I had with our Mother. I was quite happy that she could re-join her Creator and better understand the evolution she had experienced in the earthly realm. Rosemary, I wish you all the best on your journey, and I love you!

Chapter 12

The Healing Process

Once I realized that I have the power to **choose who I want to be** in every given moment, every aspect of my life and world started to materialize whatever I wanted to experience. I understood that if I wanted to feel happiness, love, joy, peace, and prosperity, all I had to do was to **choose** what I wanted to feel. I would give that feeling to someone else and immediately it was reciprocated by whomever I interacted with.

When I stopped blaming others and trying to make excuses based on external circumstances, I looked inward

The Dream of Being

and began focusing on me. I began to know the spiritual being that resides in my body, which is the vessel for my spiritual evolution.

When we are all children, we are overwhelmed with confusion and rejection; we quickly absorb the programming of our parents and the other adults in our lives. Much of that programming involves diversionary tactics—blaming someone else or something else for how one feels inside. We become programmed robots, unaware of who we truly are until we someday choose to embrace our spiritual selves once again.

Since there was no one else to blame for who I was and what I experienced in my life, I began to take responsibility. The first place I became more aware of was my household. When my husband or children would say something that evoked a negative response inside me, I would ask myself what I found threatening, and what about myself I was trying to protect. I saw that under every frustration and argument from myself was the desire to be accepted and kept safe. With this reflection, I could look back into my childhood and see how I was subconsciously connecting present events with the criticisms, rejection, and pain of my past.

As children, we had limited ways of understanding unpleasant events in our life and difficult emotions. The ego would make the best assumption it could, given the narrow scope of a child's experiences, and set up patterns that often last a lifetime. For example, if a child is rejected by his mother when he tries to be affectionate toward her, his ego will tell him to stop being affectionate—that way, he will no longer be rejected; he will be "safe." The child grows up with this pattern in place, with fears and expectations that do not necessarily serve his best interests. But because the ego tells him that his pattern keeps him safe, he will not easily step out of it or explore other alternatives. The rest of his relationships—and the rest of his life—will be affected by the faulty lessons he learned as a child. And unless he experiences significant emotional and spiritual growth, he will never even be aware of how limited he is.

With this observation in mind, every interaction I had with someone became a workshop for me. At first, I would watch our exchanges and ask myself how I felt as I automatically responded to their own mechanical speech. I realized that almost everything that anyone said or did was part of their childhood training. No one around me was authentic, nor did they realize this about themselves! It was a strange sensation, feeling as if I was constantly watching people's recorded words and behaviors just turn on and off.

When I became aware of how automated most people are, I felt as though I could never be upset or angry with anyone—everyone was doing the best that they could do with their dictated programming. Nothing—and I mean *nothing* that anyone did or said to me had anything to do with me! The negative feelings that I felt in response to people were actually just unhealed wounds that I had not yet cared for.

Therefore, when my ego—the judge of my inner hell—told me that someone was criticizing me, I would ask myself, "When did I feel criticized as a child?" A memory would always pop up in response, and I would reflect on the situation and circumstances. I would close my eyes and let myself feel what the child inside me felt, and look for why I felt that way. When I refocused my attention onto the person doing the criticizing, I would observe why they felt the need to do so—what they gained from it.

I realized that when someone was being critical of me or anyone else, they really just wanted to feel good about themselves by feeling superior. I began to look into the eyes of people who would speak ill of me or another with compassion and understanding. To be hurt by another person's words, one must actually believe that those words are true. Otherwise, the ego, as the judge of everything a person encounters, will simply dismiss those words. If I am wearing a blue blouse and someone says they like my blue blouse, my ego will subconsciously say that they are correct. If, however, someone were to say that they liked my *black* blouse, my ego would tell me that something was wrong with the person—that they were either color blind or crazy.

As individuals, we are each and every one the judge and jury of every word and action that we ever perceive. If there are fifty people observing one event, it is judged and interpreted by fifty different egos, each with different programmed reactions and perceptions. The general consensus of one's environment usually sets the standard for what is *real*, and that consensus is often determined by the media.

What I have realized is that people really want to be loved and accepted by others. They do not understand how they hurt or offend anyone unless they stop their automated speech and examine the ways that other unhealed people react to them. When older women go to the beach, they seem to spend most of their time looking down at their own bodies, noticing the changes that have taken place, rather than taking in the beauty around them. Their egos attack them with a barrage of criticism about how unattractive they have become. Their conversations reflect their feelings about themselves—not their reactions to anyone else. Like those women, we are all constantly reflecting whatever our ego is telling us at the time—our words and our actions do not say anything about anyone around us.

I was long-accustomed to automated conversation, since society demands that we follow certain habits and courtesies to comply with the standard of what is normal. I had always gone along with this way of speaking, since I wanted so much to avoid criticism in my life—I had had enough of that. But when I realized that my conversations were automated, I decided to give them meaning and purpose. I made a conscious decision that every word I spoke would be directed toward exactly what I wanted to convey, with deliberately-chosen content. No longer would I say whatever I was trained to say just so I would be accepted.

I began this journey at my last place of corporate employment. When my co-workers would say "good morning" and ask how I was doing, rather than my programmed response of "fine, thank you, how are you," I would stop and look them in the eyes and ask if they had a nice evening. At first, it was uncomfortable because I had never tried to do anything like that with meaning. The responses I got and the interactions I had, though, sent incredible positive emotions rushing through me.

Because of the positive response to this new way of talking to people, I decided to choose my words carefully so that they would always reflect who I wanted to be, instead of who my programming told me I was. I hesitated before conversing with anyone and at first, people looked at me like I couldn't hear or as if I was an idiot. However, my purpose was to experience my being at the soul level, using the words that my Creator gave me.

I wanted people to feel better after speaking with me, instead of feeling worse from the judgment and criticism that I had been trained to communicate with my words and facial expressions. Most importantly, I wanted to experience the deeper levels of love and joy that I found myself feeling after interacting with others, instead of the negative emotions I had always digested afterwards.

I realized, too, that our understanding of "wrong" is based on the idea that people *mean* to do harm—but most of us are running on automatic pilot for most of our lives, and that is when we do things that seem destructive and harmful. In reality, we are all acting out the programming we learned as children, until the point where we become self-aware and break free from our conditioning. Knowing this, I began to quiet my ego. For the first time in my life, I experienced my soul, my spirit! Feeling a deep love for and connection to humanity, I reached out and spoke to whomever I could, wherever I saw them—in the office building, in public restrooms, wherever it seemed fitting. I wanted to see who they were, and to find out what automated programming they were operating under, but I also wanted to show them that there was an alternative, that freedom was possible too. I was completely fascinated.

After some time of doing this, of letting myself be fully present with everyone in my office and the warehouse workers, some of my closest co-workers told me that people were talking about how kind and caring I was toward them. For the most part, I didn't even know some of the warehouse workers but engaged them in conversation with every opportunity that presented itself. I made it my mission to treat everyone either in the office or warehouse with reverence, as they all deserved to be treated. They had no idea that I was being filled to the brim with love and joy by being able to awaken those feelings in them.

There were times in my life that I would have paid any price to feel just an ounce of this feeling, but I did not know how or where to find it. My search was over—it was always right inside me, where my Heaven exists, and where once I could only find hell.

The Dream of Being

The hell that my Mother had ingrained into my being was extinguished by connecting with the spirit of love that resides in everyone. My compassion for others came from being able to recognize them as programmed beings who sought the same things I longed for—acceptance and love. I had a taste of enlightenment, and I now understood what it truly meant.

When I felt that I had made the changes in my thoughts and perceptions, I turned my attention to my actions: praying, cooking, cleaning, doing the laundry, even walking down the street.

No longer did I pray for God to make my life easier—I saw that "easy" is just a matter of perspective. My prayers became a conversation with my new friend, my ally, and a constant stream of giving thanks for all that I had in life. I stopped bowing my head and bending down as if I were inferior; instead, I raised my face toward the sky, knowing that God loves me unconditionally and never wanted me to feel less-than for any reason.

I thanked my new omnipresent friend for not only the obvious blessings—loved ones, money, food—but for the other measures of abundance that we often take for granted. My daily chores and housework became a work of gratitude that I have clothes and a home that can shelter me through my spiritual journey.

If I saw someone who was scarred or missing a limb, I thanked God for allowing me to experience myself in a whole body, without drastic alterations. If my body felt aches, pains, or damage, I thanked the Universe for sending me the message to change my thoughts, so I could make my body whole again. From my experiences, I know that the mind almost always controls one's illnesses and therefore, the condition of their human body.

I thanked God for the love that I could finally feel inside me, and for positive interactions with others. I no longer walked with my head down, but held it up high so that I could experience the beauty of everything around me. I breathed deeply to fill my lungs with the breath of life. For the first time, I experienced true prayer as communication with God, with a grateful heart.

I use the following example to remind myself of how I want to live my life: If I wanted to travel from my house to San Diego, I would fly on a plane and thank God for that plane. If tomorrow there were no planes to be flown, I would take a train and thank the Universe for that train. If I woke up and there were no planes or trains, I would jump into my car and thank God for my automobile. If all three ceased to exist, I would start walking to San Diego and thank God for my legs. If I woke up with no legs, I would roll through the grass and be grateful for the sunshine or the rain engulfing my being.

I have taught myself to be a constant conversation of gratitude. Every day and *everything* is a gift!

Polarities in the universe have a special meaning for our spiritual evolution—one could not experience life without polarities. We would not be able to define *tall* without *short*, or *thin* without *fat*, *hot* without *cold*, or *love* without *hatred*. I would not have known what true love is without my ego, which made me feel hatred for so long. For the first forty years of my life, my ego made me live in competition with others, believing I had to hold onto whatever I had tightly and compete for material goods— that was my idea of prosperity. If someone else did not have the right things, do the right things, or seem to be the right things, my ego judged them as *not good enough*.

Chapter 12

Dealing with the ego is not an easy task, so I knew that I needed to surround myself with the way of life that brought me the most joy. I spent my time around positive people who were interested in spiritual development. I listened to positive, uplifting music and read inspiring books; I attended spiritual retreats to further support my new perspectives.

At first, it was all too easy to fall back into my old patterns, judging and criticizing others. I became guarded and withdrew from people and situations that triggered those old thoughts. Protecting the new Heaven that I had found and cherished was my utmost priority. I grew stronger as the love inside became more constant, and I realized that I could only love others as much as I loved myself. In the past, I had believed that love was something that came from others—no wonder I never felt loved by anyone else! My ego had a long list of "do's and don'ts" that everyone had to follow in order to be *good enough* for my love, but no one can live up to the ego's standards. My ego held me hostage, feeding itself on all the negativity I had so blindly provided.

After living in an elevated state of love for almost a year, I slowly tested the waters and allowed myself to be in situations that might pull me back into a state of negativity. I still have to reassure myself each time I interact with someone who is controlled by their programming and acting out of disillusionment. I know that someone is still disillusioned when I look at them and see my own past programming in action—along with all of the negative emotions that accompany that programming, which used to control *me*.

The next step I took was to let go of the religious dogma that had provided so many rules in my life and controlled so much of my behavior. What I realized is that the rules and concepts that are written in holy books had to be interpreted by people and communicated through their individual perceptions and filters. When I researched the history behind sacred texts, I found that a lot of rules were created or changed to benefit rulers and ruling institutions—not necessarily for the good of all people. This method of controlling people still happens today, as new "sins" are identified and prohibited by religious and political leaders.

Chapter 12

The only way to captivate and control people is through fear, especially by using the threat of *hell* as the ultimate and eternal damnation. Once I moved away from anything that was fear-based or controlled by rules, I stopped worrying about the do's and don'ts of life and began to experience life with an openness to all that exists—life at its fullest. The polarities in life are meant to provide us with choices, not to control us.

This is not to say that I went out and began robbing banks, murdering, or breaking any of society's rules—I was released from my worrying, and I stopped living on pins and needles, afraid to do the wrong thing. My perception of the universe widened and I saw that there was much more beyond what my limited perspective had ever shown me.

I learned that when we become free, we are more likely to make life-affirming choices than when we feel controlled by outside forces. Authority figures use religion and morality to tap into our fears and control our actions. We are raised to believe that this is for our own good, that those authorities protect us from ourselves and from each other. But as we grow and become more enlightened, we do not need anyone else to protect us—if we rely on and trust our own spiritual guides, we discover a harmony that does not arise from control and punishment. Because we are taught not to trust ourselves, we spend our lives not trusting anyone else, and we assume that given too much freedom, people will rebel and become destructive.

Children rebel and act out when they want to assert their own will, and that rebellion is part of the child's limited array of tools with which to interact with the world. As we mature and develop spiritually, we do not have to rebel as children might, throwing tantrums and acting only in defiance. Instead, we make our choices in accord with free will, and because we are spiritual beings, the quality of our choices reflects our level of consciousness.

Freedom is nothing to be feared, and it is only the undeveloped consciousness that will seek destruction over life. The control that we think we need is both futile and impossible to maintain—the fear-based paradigms cannot hold up to the spiritual truth we all find in our hearts.

As I continued branching out in my perception of spirituality, I researched and explored spiritual prophets other than Jesus, who was the only one I had learned about growing up. I studied every subject in the "gray area" that most of society cannot comprehend, like energy and spirits on the other side, and I found my sense of self broadening and expanding with the new possibilities.

Staying confined in strict, dogmatic beliefs will stifle a person's spiritual growth. Evolving and expanding my knowledge helped me grow spiritually, and it stopped me from judging others who did not share my belief system or culture. Meeting other facets of God through those who have wisdom and beliefs that differ from your own, is both exciting and inspirational; if you are open to their unfamiliar knowledge, you can gain insight into a vast Creator.

Going to the same church every Sunday keeps a lot of people in their comfort zone, which they are afraid to step out of. I have found that everyone is looking for the same thing—love and peace—unless they are focused on feeling superior to others, with their exclusionary belief system. Open your mind and your heart, reach out of your comfort zone, and you will amazed by the parts of God that reach back to you!

The Dream of Being

For most of my life, if I could not blame another person for what went "wrong" in my life, I would blame God. When I realized that I was in control of everything that I experienced, the blaming had to stop. Our egos are brilliant at making us believe that our negative feelings are someone else's fault, but if the ego cannot find another person to hold responsible, it will point to a superior being who must be controlling everything.

Learning about and playing with energy changed all of my beliefs about the events in my life—I discovered that my world was fully formed by the energy consciousness of my mind. Two wonderful books that explain these concepts are *The Secret* by Rhonda Byrne and *The Moses Code*, by James Twyman. When I took control of my every thought, my actions then followed suit and I began to manifest the wonderful life that I knew I could have. I chose to see myself, in my mind's eye, having the experience that I longed for. I would feel the emotion that accompanied that experience and feel the effect it would have on all of humanity, and I would say out loud, "I Am That, I Am." Through this simple exercise, all manners of abundance came into my life.

Chapter 12

It is amazing to realize and experience a simple life. My Creator did not want me to experience the treasure of life as a battle of difficulties, but the complete opposite—I can enjoy Heaven on Earth. Our perception creates our reality.

There was still another obstacle for me to overcome—the greatest obstacle that a person can experience on their journey to freedom and enlightenment. The greatest force of resistance to a person's transformation is often the expectations of their family—their husband, children, siblings, and parents, especially. When a person begins to awaken their consciousness, any others who are still sleeping around her will go to great lengths to remain ignorant or to discourage that awakening, unless they wish to begin their journey too. Though they may despise the programmed person they see before them, most people find the programming more comfortable—more *safe*—than seeing someone change.

Another wonderful book that explains this process is *Awareness*, by Anthony De Mello. Being in a family, we use the word *love* to describe the conditional approval we give one another as long as everyone's words and actions align with one's own. Most people believe that their families are a source of unconditional love, and yet most people do not know what unconditional love is. At an early age, we are conditioned by our parents to be a "good boy" or a "good girl" in order to receive their love and approval. If we pick up our toys, we are rewarded with words of praise. If we draw a cute picture, we are deemed creative and, again, rewarded with approving words. Only when our behavior matches our parents' ego-based expectations do we receive the words and gestures of love and acceptance.

Through a powerful experience, I had the privilege of learning what unconditional love means to me. My youngest daughter, Julie, led me to experience emotions that I never felt with Gina. I was calmer and more peaceful when Julie was born because of what I had learned from having Gina. Larry and I were more settled, too, and we had bought our house by then and knew how much income we needed to make ends meet.

When Julie began her journey through this lifetime, I soon realized that she was unique and came into this world with fears that were not from this lifetime, including her unusual fear of men. That became apparent by the time she was nine months old, and it was not until she was five years old that Julie became comfortable around men.

During that same period of time, Julie grew very stubborn and was adamant about getting her way. If things did not go as she wanted, she would cry and scream and throw a tantrum. No amount of talking or reasoning would work with her—it was her way or the highway! I knew I could not allow her to control us, so I would take her to a safe space and allow her to go through her tantrum until she surrendered to a calm state again.

Julie was a bright child, and both school and socializing came easy to her. She made friends easily wherever she went, and she was athletically talented as well. She began playing soccer at the age of three and by the time she turned five, it was clear that she had a natural ability and intelligence beyond her years.

Since I was her soccer coach for most of her soccer career, Julie and I spent a lot of quality time together. I wished at the time that I could have a close mother-daughter relationship with Gina too, but I later understood why I did not.

The Dream of Being

When she became part of the popular circle of friends in middle school and started going to the school dances, the Julie that I knew began to change. She never wanted to be home and made up reasons to spend the night at someone else's house. There were many times that I knew she was lying about where she was going and what she was doing, but Julie was also very convincing—she could lie her way out of a paper bag. Her intelligence allowed her to run circles around anything her Dad would say, making anything she said seem logical in the end.

Even though I knew inside that things were not right in Julie's life and I feared for her, I also knew that the only thing I could do was to talk to her every chance I got, offering my guidance and reminding her that I loved her. It was time to trust in a higher power, and to trust in Julie as she directed the unfolding of her own journey.

In February of 2005, Julie joined me in the kitchen while I was preparing dinner. My spirit guide whispered in my ear, "She is going to die." It was the first time that the voice ever told me that someone was going to leave this world. I put it out of mind at the time, but later I struggled with what to do with this information, and cried at the thought of losing her. This message came at a low point in Julie's life—she was unsure of who she was and experimented with many harmful substances and behaviors. My intuition, though, told me to say nothing.

Three months later, Larry and I returned home from a weekend vacation at Lake Cumberland. I was putting things away and walked past Julie as she was getting ready in her bathroom. I stopped to listen when she said, "Oh Mom, I've got a story to tell you." She explained that she had gone canoeing with a large group of friends—it was clear that there was a lot of alcohol involved in the outing.

The friends decided to tie their two canoes together and while they were moving down the river, the canoe in front overturned. One of the young men who was in that canoe swam to Julie's and tried to climb in. While doing so, he accidentally tipped it over, sending her underwater. She tried to swim to the top, but was caught in the undertow and could not move upward. She said she eventually surrendered to the current, and saw her whole life pass before her eyes, as if a short film had been made that showed every event and every person she had experienced in her eighteen years. Out of nowhere, two hands reached down and pulled her out of the water. The young man laid her in the canoe, where she was able to finally draw in a breath again. Their eyes filled with tears as they realized what had almost happened.

When Julie finished telling her story, I looked at her with tears in my eyes and told her that the event was a warning that she was gambling with her life and that the substances she was taking were altering her authentic self. The emotions I felt inside took over, and I looked at her and softly said, "I had heard that you were going to die." To my surprise, she began yelling at me, shouting, "And you didn't say anything to me! Just shows how much you care." We looked at each other for a moment, our eyes full of tears.

As I walked away, the voice told me, "It was the best thing you could have done for her, not to tell her. You will see why shortly."

Whether or not she decided to change consciously, Julie underwent a transformation after nearly drowning. She began talking to me about living a healthier life and about staying away from certain people. Julie wanted to be different—I believe she realized that she wanted to live and not trash her being.

This was one of the most important lessons that I have ever learned in my life: If you truly love someone, love them enough to let them go so that they can decide to find their way. If I had tried to alter any part of Julie's experience, she may have stayed trapped in the dangerous web she was weaving. From this lesson, I also learned what unconditional love means—and how it feels to put my own desires for someone else aside and do what is right for them.

Shortly thereafter, Julie changed her major in college and decided to try out dental education. After a semester, it no longer appealed to her, and I suggested she work at some different places to see what she enjoyed doing. She took this advice and about a year later, she reentered college. This time, she had a much better attitude about her schooling and spent most of her time studying and working for a large financial corporation. They immediately saw her potential and began singling her out for special projects in which she excelled. At the age of twenty-three, she chose to major in Communications, with a concentration in Organizational Leadership.

When Julie began her transformation, she began dating a childhood friend of hers. Anyone who knew them or saw them together always realized that it was just a matter of time before they would date. They had energy that blended together perfectly and a sparkle came to their eyes when they were together. Their relationship is part of a life that Julie is enjoying to the fullest, which she now does in a healthy way.

I love you very much, Julie, and I cannot imagine life without you!

* Chapter 13 *

It was not until I was in my early forties that I truly fell in love with my dear husband, Larry. What I have come to realize is that I was incapable of loving him or anyone else until I learned to love myself, forgive myself, and to realize that I was not a piece of shit. The more I loved myself, the more love I had for Larry.

As I grew spiritually, I stopped demanding and requiring anything of Larry. I had no expectations of him as a husband or as a human being—whatever he wanted to do or have became fine with me. The more I felt free within myself, the more freedom I was able to give my family—freedom from the restrictions that had limited my love for them in the past.

For the first time in my life, I was in love with the man I had been married to since I was twenty years old. Beforehand, I thought I was in love with him as long as he met my expectations. This is what I was taught love was—my parents only loved me when I was "right" in their eyes, and I applied the same sense of requirement to my adult relationships.

The more I fell in love with myself, and in turn, with Larry, the less needy I became. I grew confident and realized that I did not *need* the people I cherished most in my life—my husband and my children. Instead, I *choose* to have them in my life, so I do not have to demand that they fill some void for me. I realized that I no longer had to give away part of myself to keep people in my life—I do not have to compromise myself to maintain a relationship. If the relationship is good and beneficial, I can choose to continue it as long as it is mutually healthy.

Most people do not know what true love is. They think that conditional love is true love, and call it "tough love" or claim that it is what works best for them. But we

Chapter 13

all learn what love is from our parents—and whatever we see, we imitate, subconsciously believing that it is the "right" way.

Larry began to take my breath away. I enjoyed just being with him, doing nothing. For the first time in our marriage, I felt content and did not want to *fix* us.

During my spiritual journey, Larry has continually encouraged me, telling me to do what makes me happy. He has supported me as I explored many things that he did not understand. We have still encountered some bumps along the way in this new chapter of our lives—there are still times when old emotions and old programming slips in, trying to wreak havoc.

At one time, I was visiting a man in prison whose only acquaintance was a client of mine. He needed somewhere to go after leaving prison, and I offered him my home. The only way he could come live with us was for Larry to remove all of the firearms and alcohol from the house. I asked him to take those things down the street, to our daughter's home. The way Larry reacted, you would think I had asked him to cut off one of his arms!

I believe that jealousy crept into Larry's mind and that he thought I was putting another man before him. In my mind, moving those things was a minor request, especially considering the benefit that the man would receive by having somewhere to live temporarily, rather than being on the streets. Larry and I butted heads, but I was willing to do whatever it took to help this man find a home with or without Larry. What I have come to learn is that although I treasure Larry, he cannot stop me from helping another person in a way that feels right to me. I will not choose someone else over him, but I have to follow my heart and help others as I am led to.

Larry has been a spiritual teacher for me through much of my life. He was born with so much spiritual knowledge in this lifetime, and he already understood so much that I had to comprehend through experience. However, he has admitted to learning from me as well. We have been through so much together, and we have grown stronger through every trial. I have never given up on him, and I never will. The energy we share is difficult to explain; we do not like to be apart, but we always know that a part of us remains with the other whether we are together or not. There is no doubt in my mind that Larry is my true soul mate.

Chapter 14

Removing the rules of hierarchy in my family and seeing past those in society helped me to understand that all humans are holy, not just our loved ones. I grew up being taught to respect all elders—especially my Mother and Father, aunts, uncles, and clergymen. The idea that being older meant a person automatically deserved respect was the craziest idea—even my older siblings were taught to demand respect from younger siblings, just because they were older.

Once I stopped ranking people as "more special" because of their age or title, I looked for their holiness—the spirit in everyone that is connected to the source, to our

The Dream of Being

Creator. It is especially easy to recognize in young children who are so wise, and only speak truth. Treating my children and their significant others as peers, rather than demanding respect from them, changed the dynamics of our relationships.

Being a parent is not a dictatorship. As a parent, you can offer words of wisdom, but most importantly, you set boundaries for your children and give them safe options so they can experience the freedom of making their own choices. They have to learn to exercise the innate desire for freedom that every person seeks to fulfill because sooner or later, they will demand freedom, and rebel if necessary.

Every day, I wake up and my Creator gives me a vast array of options from which to choose. I choose to experience love because I learned about the alternative from my past experiences. I would not know how to maintain the elevated state of love, or even that I *want* to, if I did not know how my choices would affect me. As our Creator nurtures us as children, we have to offer our own the freedom to make choices that are appropriate for their maturity level.

Chapter 14

No one needs any particular person in life to be whole. I choose to have the people in my life who provide me with unconditional love without judgment, and who allow me to be on the journey of my choosing. The people in our lives provide us with someone for whom we can feel love or hate as we choose. Our family members may provide us with the positive, loving support we need on our journey, or we can create a non-biological family with equal or greater closeness. However, we do not owe anyone anything because of when and where we are born—everyone is family!

It is our ego that makes us think we *know* things—but we are put on this Earth to be students of the Universe. The only way to grow and to find happiness is by humbling ourselves and letting life teach us something better than the robotic programming our parents hand down to us.

I have known many people in my life, and through my holistic business in particular, who refuse to be helped. They come into my office and tell me something is bothering them. I ask them why it bothers them, and they always say that someone else should not be doing what makes them feel this way. When I ask about their childhoods to discover the underlying reason for their unhappiness, they refuse to discuss it, saying their parents never did anything wrong.

People are loyal to their parents and often feel threatened by the idea that their childhood was not perfect and may have left scars. If they admit that it was not always rosy, they seem to think they are betraying their loved ones. Even after I was married, I can recall believing that my childhood was perfect and that there was nothing wrong with how my parents raised me. It was easy for me to think this way for many years—until I dealt with the child inside me, who indeed did have plenty of pain and hurt growing up.

We make ourselves believe that whatever we experienced was "normal," just a regular, healthy part of childhood. I recall doing a reading for a man and asking him if he was abused as a child. Adamantly, he told me, "No, I wasn't." I then asked him if his father would beat him and hit him with wood. "Yeah," he said, "but that was normal." I asked him if he had enjoyed being treated that way as a seven year-old boy, and he said, "No, but I deserved it." Sitting in his seat, he began to cry.

We have to realize that we are not betraying or criticizing our parents by acknowledging the truth about how they programmed us. We all have issues from childhood that need to be addressed; if you think that you do not, you are disillusioned and cannot begin to awaken—you cannot obtain the peace that we all yearn for inside ourselves. Become your own best friend—you are connected to God and possess all the answers you will ever need.

Observe yourself on a daily basis. Listen to your thoughts, the words you speak, and your actions. Do they reflect the God inside you, or do they reflect what your ego tells you to do to be accepted by society? Do not let society make you a puppet—experience this lifetime as the evolution it is, and let the Creator lead your way!

Once you surrender, divine intervention takes hold.

Spreading the Light

Personal Experiences with Lois

About five years ago, I was going through a very emotional and difficult divorce, and worked for a verbally abusive boss. My relationship with my family was constantly up and down and I felt that I had spent my whole life trying to please everyone, and yet no one ever seemed happy. I had spent twenty-plus years in traditional therapy battling depression, but nothing seemed to help. One day, at my lowest point, I took a handful of pills and tried to end it all. Fortunately, my best friend found me

The Dream of Being

and by the time I reached the hospital, they told her that another hour and I would have been gone.

Shortly after this time, a friend of mine introduced me to Lois; we went to her for a reading. During the reading, Lois was able to pick up on some of the issues I had experienced and offered so much encouragement, unconditional acceptance and love that I had never felt from anyone. She was not there to judge me or to ask anything from me, as so many people in my past had. Lois was there to help me and to show me the way to the inner peace that I had searched for my whole life. She has taught me that I do have a purpose on this earth and I was allowing others to get in my way of finding it. Lois reminded me that when my time on earth is done, and I reach the other side, I only have to account for my actions on earth, how I lived my life—not the act of spinning my wheels, trying to make others happy and giving them what they wanted or needed.

Since meeting Lois, my life has taken a new direction. Yes, there are still days that I get a bit off track, but it takes a little while to undo all of the traditional programming I learned for more than forty years of my life. I now take the time to stop and thank the universe for all of my blessings, and to see how fortunate I am. More importantly, I know that whenever I am going through a rough situation, I know that the universe is trying to teach me something through it and I know I will be okay.

I now have a beautiful one year-old son who means everything to me. If I had not met Lois and had given up, I would not have him in my life—I would not have found my purpose.

~ B., Northern KY

*

I met Lois about two years ago. Lois has had such a positive impact on my life ever since. I lost my parents at the young age of twelve years old. Lois was able to help me reconnect with them. I thought it was totally impossible to get to know them after all these years. I know this may sound strange but I've been able to have a relationship with them beyond the grave.

Lois has taught me that dying is not so scary and that our deceased loved ones are only one dimension above us and they see everything going on in our lives. Lois has helped me with my business also. I use her as a life coach. I don't make any important decision without running it past Lois first! Lois has been a Godsend. I'm extremely grateful for having her in my life.

~ Diane W.

*

Lois Giancola. She teaches the alchemy of turning darkness to light within your own spirit, emotion, and perception. She has shown me the liberation and fulfillment of living my honest, authentic self in every moment. Lois empowers me with acute self-awareness and with her guidance I have been shown time and again how the energy I put into the world determines what comes back to me. I have never seen such unwavering compassion and insight. She is unconditional Truth, Light, and Love. My heart is waking up to a most beautiful and magical reality. I am forever thankful.

~Courtney Louise

*

Lois has been a gift from heaven for me and for my family. My husband and I adopted three children with severe early childhood trauma and deep emotional challenges. After discovering that we could not parent them the same as we did our biological children, we found ourselves desperate for help. Traditional services did not work for these kids. We became more frustrated and hopeless. We were experiencing our own trauma. With the help and guidance of Lois and her kind heart, we were able to help these children so they could live normal lives. Beyond that, she was such a great influence on me.

She was instrumental in helping me start my second career—earning certifications in natural healing techniques that I learned from Lois—and now I am able to help challenging children and their families all over Northern Kentucky. The greatest result is to have her as a forever friend. Lois is truly a gift to this world and an inspiration to all that meet her and know her. She exceeds all expectations! Good wishes and congrats to Lois!

~ Lynn Griffith, Director, Sunshine Ranch at Shady Hollow; Burlington, KY

What can I say? She is amazing. I first met Lois at a friend's house. I was invited for a group reading. I did not take it seriously as I had met several psychics in the past and assumed she was the same. Boy, was I wrong! First of all, she is not a psychic, she is a medium. Big difference. I also assumed a group reading would be meaningless; after all, how would she be able to distinguish between all of the participants? I was one of approximately eight and I was the first to go as I had to leave for an appointment.

I do not remember much, but I do remember the two main things she told me. She mentioned that my Dad was ill, terminally ill. And he was. She also mentioned that she saw "2" and didn't know if that meant he had two months, two years or what. Well, he was terminally ill, but had been in remission, or so we thought. So, I wasn't concerned because I was in denial. I assumed that he would live for quite awhile. Well, around two months later, he passed. I was shocked. But, I did not think about what Lois had said at that time.

At the group reading, she also mentioned something about an affair taking place between two people at my

Spreading the Light

place of employment. I really dismissed this as being almost impossible, to the point that the next day, one of my co-workers and I actually had a good laugh about it. Well, lo and behold, around six months later, we discovered that an affair between two employees had been going on and everyone was completely shocked. I reminded my co-worker of our conversation six months earlier and we were amazed!

After that, I believed Lois. I saw her several more times for readings with groups and one-on-one. She helped me to communicate with my Dad on the other side. She helped me to heal and through our readings, she helped my Mother and Sister too.

I have a niece that was having some issues living in a haunted dorm at college. There was a rather unfriendly, scary spirit, who had not crossed over and was bothering my Niece and trying to do some bad things to her. Lois actually came out with me to campus and we met in my Niece's room. She was able to make sure that this spirit stayed out of her room and left her alone. Because of Lois, my Niece could focus on school again and was no longer scared. At one point we thought she may have to move to another dorm or apartment mid-year, which isn't easy, but thanks to Lois, she made it through the rest of the year with no further problems. It was quite an experience.

Because of my experiences with Lois, I have referred her to many friends and family for readings. She is now helping my Aunt who recently lost her husband. My friends and family have had AMAZING stories to tell me about their awesome experiences with Lois.

I am proud to call Lois a friend. Many people are afraid to visit mediums because they are skeptical, leery and downright scared. But, Lois is so caring and so normal—like a good friend to everyone.

~ Judy

*

I first met Lois when I went to her for a flame-card reading with some of my friends from work in 2004. She had worked at the same company as my husband for a brief time. He told me that she was a psychic/medium and some of his co-workers had already received some amazing readings from her and suggested I go as well.

Spreading the Light

I was a little leery and nervous at first, but was very curious and eager to see what information she would hit on. At the time, I did believe in psychics and mediums, but deemed very few people had this gift and the fact that I didn't really know Lois made me question her abilities. Little did I know I would be blown away with her accuracy. I had always thought my family members who passed were still with me, but little did I know they would communicate with me from the other side.

My father came through during my first reading. Lois said my father was adamant that I had a photograph of him in his cowboy hat. I recalled seeing a picture of him wearing a cowboy hat when I was younger but was confident I did not own it. Lo and behold, when I returned home that evening, I found the picture of my father wearing his cowboy hat in the first album I checked. I could hardly believe it but it did make me a true believer in Lois.

Over the next few years, I continued to get readings from Lois and was always astounded at the accuracy of information she would pour out. I couldn't help asking myself, "How could she know this about me if I never told

The Dream of Being

her?" However, she never disappointed and her predictions were dead on, even if I didn't always accept or believe them right away.

One reading in particular stands out for me that really changed my life. If it weren't for Lois, I would never have shaken the guilt about the way my father died. My father died alone on Thanksgiving weekend in his home on his bed and was found with the phone off the hook as he attempted to call for help. The sadness and guilt I felt over the years were overwhelming since I had not gone to visit him that weekend although I knew he was ill. For years, I couldn't talk about my father's death without tearing up.

Then, one day during a reading, Lois hit the nail on the head. She said, "You have a problem with your father's death or the way he died." I was shocked since I had only shared this with one other person and there is no way she could have known this about me.

I agreed with her and she went on to relay a message from my father saying, "He said it was okay and he doesn't want you to be sad about this anymore. He was not alone since your mother and his other family members on the other side were there for him." For the first time in fifteen years, I felt relieved and at peace with the way he passed. It was a turning point in my life and only the beginning of the journey Lois has taken me on.

Recently, I have taken classes from Lois on how to develop my own intuition abilities and am truly amazed at how much I've learned from her. In the beginning, I had doubts that I could develop my intuition ability but Lois proved me wrong. Through her classes, Lois taught me how to get answers for myself from my spirit guides whenever I need guidance in my daily life. The stress in my life has been greatly reduced since I've been using these techniques. Lois has empowered me and I am forever grateful to her. She is a wonderful spirit and such an inspiration and I know she will continue to inspire others in this life and the next.

~ Kathy Donoghue, Cincinnati, Ohio

*

I met Lois through my sister; they worked together at Toyota years ago. When Sue told me about Lois I was skeptical, especially about mediums talking to dead people. I had lost my first husband because of a

The Dream of Being

motorcycle accident in 1990, and remarried four years later. I lived a life where I thought I was happy, at least some of the time, for 14 years.

My children and granddaughters brought me much joy and one day in April almost two years ago, I found out my husband was accused of molesting my granddaughter, who at the time was almost five. He was convicted and went to jail, and I was in disbelief. How could I have been married to someone for that long and not see anything? My granddaughter loved him so much.

I had seen Lois off and on for a period of years for life coaching, EFT, and mediumship. I have issues with self-confidence, but while I was in Lois's office, I would feel so good talking to her, I felt like I could conquer the world—she just has a way of making you feel so good and loved. She brings things out that may be hard to face and I felt like fifty-six years of my life were a big lie. I was conditioned to always be good, and don't make waves. Now I know it was all an act, that I wasn't true to myself... hell, I didn't even know what that meant.

It has been a battle to change and become who I want to be, but I am making strides. I am going through a long, drawn-out divorce and trying to sell my house, but I got a new full-time job, which I haven't had since I was eighteen years old. Through a lot of hard work I know I will get there. I tell Lois all the time if I could handcuff her to me I could do anything. She is such an inspiration to my daughters and me—we truly love her.

It totally freaks me out when she talks to my relatives on the other side. I am not a skeptic any longer, and I believe in what she does wholeheartedly. She truly is a gift from God, and I thank him every day for her.

~ Anonymous

*

I have had many wonderful experiences with Lois Giancola. I have several instances where her intuitive nature has helped guide me through difficult decision-making situations within my career and personal life. I have also experienced Lois's personal commitment to helping me through past experiences, which brought me some peace and understanding regarding an issue that happened over forty years ago.

The Dream of Being

I'd like to offer the following testimony as support to Lois's ability in several areas:

I had asked Lois to help me overcome a childhood experience which I found difficult to work through. I had no idea how it was affecting me throughout my life. With Lois's help, I felt an acceptance that the situation did happen and her guidance helped me to appreciate how the situation has created the person I am today. I felt such wonderful peace when I left that session with Lois, that it seemed people could feel the peaceful energy coming from me for several days following the visit.

Without any knowledge of what I was going through at work, Lois called me early one morning and told me I was going to be experiencing difficult days. Several times, I had to stand up for what I believed was right and hold my ground with superiors. This normally would have been extremely difficult for me, but with the support of Lois's guidance I was able to feel strength and confidence. Both times Lois was absolutely correct with her predictions of the day's events.

Another example of Lois's ability to predict an upcoming event occurred when Lois called me to see how

I was doing and I told her my son's car had been stolen. We had reported it stolen the day before. She told me she felt the car would be recovered in good condition and it would be in a parking lot. Because of my faith in Lois, I asked her if something of sentimental value would still be in the trunk. She said it would be there. Two days later, the police called to report the car had been found in a parking lot. When my Son got there to identify it, the police opened the trunk and his golf clubs were still there. I was able to support my son through the difficult days because I held on to what Lois told me.

When you trust in her ability, it allows you to go through difficult times with peace and confidence.

~ Maggie Morande

*

I have known Lois all of my life. She married my mom's brother. I would see her at family parties and holidays, but I was never very close with anyone in my family. I started using and drinking at a pretty early age, and had the alcoholic/addict behaviors and thought patterns way before I ever picked up.

The Dream of Being

I moved to the Cleveland, Ohio area for about five years, and ended up with a child and an abusive fiancé (who soon became my ex-fiancé). I moved back to my old Kentucky home, dragging a three-year old daughter along, determined to try and make a good life for us. I started attending college, worked part-time, and lived at my parents'. I didn't like it, but I was okay with it for the time. The longer I was home, the more hopeless, resentful, and lost I started to feel. And I found my way to escape was by drinking and drugging. Within three years of moving home, I was addicted to opiates and alcohol. Then I moved on to methadone.

I had been using methadone daily for a year when I finally decided that I wanted to stop. But by then I was physically addicted (as well as mentally and emotionally). The pain and sickness that followed were more than I could handle on my own. So I continued to use methadone for another year. That was the worst year of my life. I knew that I was in serious trouble. I was sick all the time, either from not having enough drugs in my system or from too many. I knew that I couldn't stop using on my own, but that I couldn't let my family know how much trouble I

Spreading the Light

was in. I had managed to keep my parents in the dark about my drug use, and I had become isolated from everyone except the person I was using with. I felt totally alone and lost. I was trapped inside this disease, not knowing that I actually had a disease, and the disease was trying to kill me.

It was Labor Day, which meant that everyone would be coming over for the fireworks. I was trying to get myself together to be able to handle this mob of family. I was alone upstairs when everyone started to arrive. I tried to stay hidden, but that didn't work out like I had planned. Lois came into the room and started to talk to me. She had heard my great-grandma (we all called her Gram) tell her to talk to me. And that's how it all came out that I was an addict and in a whole lot of trouble! From that day, Lois helped me find other people and places that could help me. I eventually found a treatment center in Tennessee that would take me. So all that was left was for me to tell my parents, and Lois was kind enough to be with me for that, too.

I have since completed a ninety-day stint in a treatment center, and I am so happy to be coming up on six months of sobriety! I truly believe that if Lois would not have been open and able to hear what she heard that day, I would either be dead or still addicted to methadone (which is comparable to being one of the walking dead).

I am currently taking an intuition class from Lois. This class and the things I am learning in it are helping me develop and maintain a relationship with my higher power. I am learning how to honor my own energy, and tap into the universe. And these are things that help me keep some perspective in sobriety.

~ Rachel S.

*

My name is Cheryl, and I am so grateful for meeting Lois, her friendship, and the healing she has brought to me over the past year. On February 19, 2009, I witnessed a horrible accident on I-74 on my way to work at 5:30 a.m. on a very icy morning. A man lost control of his car and slid sideways in the middle of the highway. He got out of his car and walked to the shoulder of the road to call for help and to get away from his car. A white truck was coming down the highway, swerved away to miss his car, and hit him head-on. His body buckled over the hood of the truck. It didn't seem real, this scene that I just witnessed. I was horrified, but called 911. Soon, I found out that the man had died.

I went to work and was sick to my stomach all day. All I could think about was his family, that scene, and the person who hit him and how they felt. It played over and over in my mind... and I had to drive past the place it occurred every day. I started having dreams about people dying, and couldn't get over this sick feeling. I started to see a therapist and that helped a little, but never really helped ease the sadness. A woman at work said I should go talk to Lois, that maybe she could help.

I had never met her before, she didn't know me, or why I was there. She talked to me about my family, and told me things no one else would know, so I was impressed right away. Then she said, "You witnessed a horrible accident." I couldn't believe it! She said the man was there and wanted to tell me that he was fine, and he appreciated my concern, my compassion, and my calling for help that day. He assured me that he felt no pain. He said it was simply his time to leave this world, and I should not feel sad. Lois held my hand and did EFT, saying I would not be sad anymore, that I will have good thoughts about this place when I drive past, and I will see this as a positive experience. I have had a weight lifted from me since that day forward, and am at peace about this whole situation. It truly changed my life!

~Cheryl, Indiana

*

What can I say to describe the transformative impact that Lois has had on my life? I may describe my change as a 360-degree turn. She has been such a friend, a mentor, an avatar, a magician, a spiritual director, a confessor and a soul sister. Her strong connection to spirit has given her grounding as well as a force to urge the growth of all who have had the privilege to experience her gifts.

Her classes encouraged individuation. We were able to look at life with new eyes. We were able to view the world with new perceptions, truths that our souls recognized as being our truths. I was at a point in life where the world's solutions, handed down by school, family, church and society, just didn't fit. It was time for me to "grow up" again, in new skin. I wasn't a puppet in my own life but a living, breathing soul. Being my more authentic self, my life and loves are more vibrant. Lois encouraged growth, never forcing her ideas, but she was there to love and encourage my own transformation.

Her different modalities—Reiki, EFT, intuition, mediumship—all center on spirit and empowering souls to the highest life that we can attain while on earth school. I was truly honored (and again transformed) by her officiating and blessing my wedding. I have witnessed so many personal miracles through Lois that I have become accustomed to the extraordinary life we are meant to experience.

~ Beth Funyak

*

In early 2009, I had a Vedic astrology reading done; I had wanted to get one for about two years, but had not set aside the money for it until I got my tax refund sometime that February. The woman who did the reading recommended EFT to me, as I mentioned to her that I have

The Dream of Being

been underweight for quite a while, and that I thought there was an emotional or psychological reason for it.

Until this point, I had tried every kind of therapy—alternative and conventional—I could find. I was seeing a therapist who was doing a certain cognitive therapy (called EMDR) on me to help my brain process old memories and properly store them. I only used herbal medicine, but had taken anti-depressants and other medications in the past. I drank a lot. I had worked with crystals and was certified as a Reiki master, and had also given myself a number of scars from dragging a razor blade across my skin so I could feel the pain. I was a single mother with two children, renting a house that was as dark and falling apart as I felt inside.

So I started researching EFT—I was willing to try anything that might help me get some relief from the despair I felt. I found the website of the man who first introduced the technique, Gary Craig, and tried to do EFT on myself, but all of the success stories I read made me want to find an experienced practitioner. I searched for EFT providers in Kentucky and found two listed; Lois Giancola's website said that she was willing to be flexible with financial arrangements. Since I was working a part-time job and barely had enough income to make it through each month, I called her.

When I arrived for my first appointment, I was hopeful that EFT would work for me, but I was also skeptical of Lois, which I thought was important to keep me from being naïve. (Ironically, I have seldom been skeptical of truly deceptive people in my life.) I felt so angry in general, and so distrustful, and I know now that Lois must have seen all of that right away. When she asked me what I wanted to work on, I did not know what to tell her. She asked me to tell her my two most traumatic memories and I did. She used EFT on me to help me address the trauma associated with those memories, and when I left, I felt like I had more freedom in my body than I ever had before.

My beloved grandmother was dying at that time. She was the only person in my life who had told me I was special. I felt safe around her, and her love for me was part of my glimmer of hope in an otherwise desperate life. Lois assured me that a lot of my anger at that time was related to knowing that my Granny was dying. I didn't believe her, as I thought I was dealing with her deteriorating health sensibly and logically.

At my Granny's funeral, I cried and cried, but in a few visits with Lois, I had come to understand how much I adored my Granny, how much I had needed her, and how willingly she had helped me throughout my life. She was an incredible blessing to me, and I was a blessing to her. Though I was sad to not have her any more, I was able to accept that it was time for her to move on, and I came to understand just how much I treasure her.

Though I did not realize it at the time, Lois gave so much to me throughout that entire experience. She listened to me patiently, even though so much of what I said reflected my mindset at the time—I felt sorry for myself and my sad life, but I did not think that any of my misery had anything to do with my actions, my beliefs, or my sense of self. Although I knew I had sabotaged some parts of my life, and that I was surely affected by my abusive upbringing, I was still convinced that I was a victim of circumstances and of other people. With kindness and compassion, Lois helped me see that *all* of my problems came from something within me—my beliefs, my expectations, and my own self-destructive choices. Knowing that was overwhelming, and I felt waves of guilt and shame each time I became more aware of how I had sabotaged my own life. But I also realized that if all of my problems started with me, I could change my life by changing myself—and that thought showed me a way out of the hell that completely enveloped me.

I started seeing Lois on a weekly basis, and I began the intense, difficult process of becoming more self-aware. Two of my greatest teachers were already right beside me: my one year-old daughter and my eight year-old son. I thought of myself as a good mother, and in ways, I was. I provided the best food I could to my children. We did not spend a lot of time with the television on. I gave them books and read to them a lot. They were always clean and well-dressed.

And yet, I knew that my anger had to be affecting them. I yelled fairly often, and sometimes I was downright mean. I was hardly ever patient when my son made normal childish "mistakes," and my tone of voice could make him cry.

I had plenty of excuses on hand, though. I was so stressed. I was worried about money. I felt betrayed by a friend. My exes were thoughtless. The yard needed to be mowed. There were ants in the kitchen. The basement was flooded and the dishes needed to be done and I was embarrassed to have people over and I was all alone and I had no idea how I was going to make it and on and on.

My son had issues with bullies for years at the various schools he has attended. I always tried to be the good parent, called the teachers, talked with my son about how to respond to the kids, and so on. One teacher suggested that he was lying to get my attention, and I dismissed the idea—I gave him plenty of attention! Shortly after he turned nine, he was accused of bullying smaller kids in his martial arts class, and the question that had been nagging me for so long finally demanded to be asked: What part did I play in the bullying in his life?

When I finally asked myself that question, I felt like crawling under a rock and hiding for the rest of my life. I did not feel that I deserved to be a mother, or even to be alive any more. I felt that I had failed my son, that I had ruined his life, and that I had shown myself as being no better than my parents had been toward me. I was horrified. The guilt and shame were almost unbearable.

Over the next couple of days, I prayed that the suffering I was experiencing would turn out to be an important and powerful lesson, that I could feel okay again someday, armed with my new understanding. I saw Lois a couple of times and she suggested I wear a rubber band around my wrist and snap it when I felt angry toward my children, and she also suggested taking three deep breaths before speaking.

I did look for a rubber band at home and did not find one immediately. Taking deep breaths always seemed too cliché for me, so I did not try that either. At my next appointment, I told her about losing my temper with my son once again after he claimed that a little girl threw a ball at his face. When he told me that, I felt like there was absolutely nothing I could do to protect him or teach him; I had no idea how to give him the tools he needed to stand up for himself. So I yelled at him and was once again rude and hurtful, though I told myself I had done my best and there was nothing else I could do about this pattern in his life.

Immediately after that happened, I served our dinner but could not sit down and eat with my children. I was so frustrated and full of anxiety that I did not want to be in the same room with them. I went into my bedroom and sat down on my bed and asked my spirit guides to show me the right thing to do and how to handle the situation that had unfolded. I knew right away that I needed to apologize and ask for my son's forgiveness. I also realized that my reaction reflected my own self-loathing and a persistent sense of inadequacy—which showed me the next, most important, personal work I needed to do.

When I apologized, explained myself, and asked for my son's forgiveness, he said he could not forgive me at that time. I felt like the child suddenly, desperate for his acceptance. But I just said that I understood, and I spent the rest of the evening cuddling with him and watching one of his favorite television shows. At the end of the night, he told me he forgave me, and I thanked him. I asked him if he was sure he felt ready, and he said he was. I let him sleep in my bed that night, as he asked to do, and I gave thanks that he was still a little boy who wanted to cuddle and watch television together.

Our relationship was not damaged beyond repair, and I had the chance to regain his trust. The experience strengthened my commitment to overcoming the anger and pain I have long carried inside me.

Like many people, my anger and pain has everything to do with my childhood. My father was particularly abusive, and my mother either turned her head or was too busy trying to survive to protect her children. In many ways, I am nothing like them. In some ways, I am just like them. I have had to learn—through some damn hard lessons—what it means to have self-control, to take responsibility for my life, to manage my life, and to be a parent.

It is so worth it. When I was apologizing to my son for losing my temper, I told him that I know I am not perfect, and nobody is, but that I am committed to doing whatever it takes to have less anger. He said, "Oh you have gotten a lot better—you are a lot less angry than you used to be." And I am.

As a teenager, I was filled with rage and did not know how to cope with it. I tried every drug that I could find until shortly before I became pregnant with my son. For most of my adulthood, I drank a bit too much. I smoked cigarettes off and on, but mostly on, for almost a decade. Now I do not do any of those things, and the anger inside of me has become weaker and weaker. At the same time, my confidence in myself and in the goodness of life has become stronger. With each day that passes, I know that I am closer to achieving my every dream, and to filling my life with positivity and joy.

At the next appointment I had with Lois after the incident with my son, I gave her my excuse for not having a rubber band around my wrist: I could not find one. We talked, and she did EFT on me for a few issues I was concerned about, including my patience with my children. When I came home after work the next day, there was a green rubber band lying on my kitchen counter. It had to be for me, so I said a quick "thank you" and put it around my wrist. I started taking the three deep breaths, too, and found that it relieved a lot of my tension.

I snapped the rubber band a few times, and it helped remind me each time that I am more interested in having good relationships with my children than I am about being right, or them being perfectly obedient, or them doing everything I want without fail. I was raised with those kinds of demands, and I never measured up. It has been easy to feel helpless when I realize how I have repeated the terrible lessons of my parents. But I have found my way out, and I am making my way further each day into the life that reflects my deepest values and my greatest dreams.

One day, I told a friend that I was really looking forward to my appointment with Lois. He responded, "Dependent?" It sounded like a question, but it seemed that he was implying there was something unhealthy about how good I felt when I went to see Lois. I asked myself if I was using her as a crutch, or if I had become needy and clingy with her, as I had in past relationships. I thought about it for a good long while, and waited for the disappointing truth that I was sure would come. In the end, though, I realized that none of my behavior reflected an unhealthy dependence.

When I listened to whatever Lois had to say, I invariably felt like she was telling me something that I already knew, but that I had never put into words. Or sometimes, it seemed that she was just reminding me of something that I had thought before, but which had faded into the background of my mind. I needed to meet and work with Lois like I need sunshine and air—to help me grow and become my best self. We all need help in this life, whether it is apparent or not. We learn so much from each other and have the capacity for limitless growth. Unhealthy dependence might temporarily delay our growth, but the human spirit can be derailed and delayed for only so long.

I started seeing Lois because I knew I needed something. I had been searching high and low since I was fifteen years old and still had not found it; now I have two children who need me to find my own inner peace. I think that some relief from my pain was necessary for myself alone, but my children remind me so often of what is hurting inside me—they make it impossible to ignore.

I did not go into Lois's office thinking that EFT was going to work for me. I was skeptical of a lot of the spiritual principles she talked about, though I was willing to give them a try. Now I realize that Lois saw me more clearly than I saw myself, and she showed me what it means to love someone unconditionally. She has treated me with love always because it is what we are meant to do—not because she wanted to "save" me, nor because she pitied me or wanted something in return. She helped me feel safe so I could let down my defenses and be ready to make the changes I so desperately needed to make. She encouraged me and gave me guidance with complete honesty, and my shame, guilt, and fear melted away. And Lois has asked nothing of me. We have chosen to do projects together, but she does not expect me to be or do or say anything that does not work for me.

I have been looking for answers all my life, searching for anything that would make me feel *okay* in this world. Since I met Lois, I have made vast improvements in my life and in my relationships. It has been a lot of work, but the rewards have been infinitely greater. I see my ideal life within my reach, and just knowing that makes all the work worthwhile.

I have no idea how my life would have gone if I had not gotten the guidance and healing I needed, but I am certain that I would be in a much darker place. Worst of all, I would not even know why life felt so hard all the time. My journey has taken a beautiful turn, and I am grateful that Lois is part of that.

~ Bobi Conn, Berea, Kentucky

About the Author

Lois Giancola, HHCP, is a Medium, a Board Certified Holistic Counselor & Practitioner, Life Coach and a Reiki Master. She combines these and other modalities to provide integrated holistic healing services to the public. Her business is based in Northern Kentucky, but the effects of her work reach beyond any geographical borders.

Lois spent much of her life living an illusion, stuck in the same kind of nightmare that so many people feel trapped in. When she realized she could no longer live the same life she had grown accustomed to, she began her search for meaning and direction. She found her way to authentic living, and now helps others find their own authentic selves. Anyone wishing to contact Lois may do so through her website, www.loisgmedium.com.

About the Co-Author/Editor

Bobi Conn is a writer who currently lives in Berea, Kentucky, with her two children. She enjoys writing in a variety of genres, and this represents her first co-authoring

The Dream of Being

project. She has also written a literary memoir, several short stories, and many poems.

She currently teaches Creative Writing and Women's Studies at Eastern Kentucky University as a part-time instructor. Bobi is enthralled with learning, and is an avid student of child development, horticulture, cooking, spiritual growth, and more.

Co-authoring this book was an honor for her, and she has found her experiences with Lois Giancola and the writing of this book to be profoundly transformative.

Made in the USA
Charleston, SC
03 June 2013